DE LA SOUL

ADDITIONAL TITLES

Brainiac by Justin Vellucci

AFI by Andi Coulter

DE LA SOUL

Dave Heaton

J-Card Press

COPYRIGHT © 2024 BY DAVE HEATON

All rights reserved. This book or any portion thereof may not be reproduced or used in any manner whatsoever without the express written permission of the publisher except for the use of brief quotations in a book review.

ISBN: 979-8-9891947-6-6 (print)
ISBN: 979-8-9891947-7-3 (ebook)

Library of Congress Control Number: 2024936503

J-Card Press
460 Center Street #6578
Moraga, California 94570

Cover photo by Matti Hillig
Interior design by Dan Stuckie
Author photo by Chandler Johnson

www.jcardpress.com

CONTENTS

1. Bigger than Me: An introduction **1**

2. Different, but Dope:
Youth culture and the members of De La Soul **9**

3. Believe What We Believe:
Getting started, getting signed, and the first singles **27**

4. Eyes Wide Open:
3 Feet High and Rising and the D.A.I.S.Y. Age **41**

5. Shades of Black Complexity:
The Native Tongues collective **67**

6. Trying to Still Live:
Controlling the narrative through *De La Soul Is Dead* **77**

7. Through the Machine:
Buhloone Mindstate and growing up **95**

8. What's Going On:
The turning point that was *Stakes Is High* **111**

9. That New-Millennium Feel:
The *Art Official Intelligence* "trilogy" **121**

10. Legacy Lives On:
Industry turmoil, *Grind Date*, and Gorillaz **131**

11. Stars Unleashed:
The digital void and the *Anonymous Nobody* **139**

12. Creativity Does Flourish:
Reissues, tragedy, and the future **149**

13. Up in My Head Right Now: A conclusion **157**

Acknowledgments 161

Chapter Notes 163

BIGGER THAN ME:
AN INTRODUCTION

The graffiti writer tells his DJ friend that their art is about living for today: "Tomorrow's a long way off, man. When I'm writing trains or when you're mixing sounds, making people dance, that's everything. We're alive!"

That's a scene from the movie *Beat Street*. Released in the summer of 1984, the same weekend as *Ghostbusters* and *Gremlins*, it was one of Hollywood's first attempts to make mass entertainment (money) out of the New York City scene that by that point was *the* means of expression among young people living in the city and its surroundings—and had started spreading to urban youth across the United States. *Beat Street* was the Hollywoodized capitalization on *Wild Style*, the first hip-hop film. Filmed in '81 and '82, and released theatrically in '83, that low-budget film was closer to the scene in every sense—starring real-life participants in the music, graffiti, and breakdancing scene of the time.

Hip-hop as a musical and cultural phenomenon is considered to have started in August 1973, with Kool Herc DJing his sister Cindy Campbell's house party in the Bronx. A decade later, the country overall was waking up to its existence and turning it into a commercial proposition.

In the early eighties, breakers were showing up in movies (*Flashdance, Breakin'*) and in TV commercials for products as big as Pepsi and McDonald's. Breakers were treated as a novelty, but also represented a visual manifestation of the youth culture that had taken over New York City, the nation, and eventually the world.

About seven minutes in movie time after the "we're alive" conversation, *Beat Street*'s graffiti writer character, Ramon "Ramo" Franco (played by Jon Chardiet), dies a tragic death on electrified subway tracks. The movie's climax is a New Year's Eve party turned memorial tribute for Ramo, with an atmosphere of both mourning and joy. The DJ character proclaims, "It's not gonna be a funeral, it's a celebration." The scene was set and filmed at a club that the real musicians and breakdancing crews in the movie (Afrika Bambaataa & Soulsonic Force, Treacherous Three, Grandmaster Flash and the Furious Five, Rock Steady Crew, New York City Breakers) knew well: the Roxy, which was located in the Chelsea neighborhood of Manhattan. The movie version of the club is the setting for a joyous memorial celebration. Blue-and-silver-robed gospel singers, led by Bernard Fowler, turn the club into church. The film's main characters stand within a crowd on the stage. They laugh, hug, and dance through their tears.

March 2, 2023, a real-life event has a similar mixture of celebration and grief. Vincent Mason Jr., a.k.a. DJ Maseo of the rap trio De La Soul, is on stage at Webster Hall, in the East Village of Manhattan, about a mile and a half from where the Roxy once stood. Maseo is struggling to find the words to sum up how he feels, eighteen days after the death of fellow De La Soul founding member David Jude Jolicoeur, who went by Trugoy the Dove and then simply by

Dave. "My emotions are very displaced," he says. "My man is gone..."

That night Mason was surrounded on stage by friends: Kelvin Mercer a.k.a. Posdnuos of De La Soul, Prince Paul, Queen Latifah, Monie Love, Dres of Black Sheep, Common, Talib Kweli, Busta Rhymes, comedian Dave Chappelle, and more. Those individuals represented the sweep of De La Soul's career and success, from their early singles in the late eighties through their status as influential mentors for a younger generation of artists.

The event was planned before Jolicoeur's death at age fifty-four from heart failure shocked the hip-hop world. The night labeled the D.A.I.S.Y. Experience was intended to be sheer celebration. De La Soul's first six albums were finally appearing on a music streaming service, that night at midnight, after two decades of legal and contractual battles eliminated the chances that new listeners would find their way to the group's most significant recordings. The New Year's Eve–style countdown was to a new era of availability, a world where De La Soul's music had reemerged from the void.

It wasn't easy for the now-duo of De La Soul—Mercer and Mason, Posdnuos and Maseo, Plug 1 and Plug 3—to get in a celebratory mood for the occasion. In a July 2023 video interview with Lyndsey Parker of Yahoo Entertainment, Mason gave Mercer credit for pulling him out of his funk and convincing him that the show must go on. "He came up with the greatest idea that I thought was perfect. 'He was our Ramon.... We need to celebrate this, like the New Year's Eve party in *Beat Street*.'"

In the week leading up to the D.A.I.S.Y. Experience, it was reframed as a tribute to Dave: "Join us to celebrate the life and legacy of Dave aka Plug 2 and De La Soul."

Dave's death, and the De La Soul streaming launch, came during a commemorative year for hip-hop: nominally the fiftieth year of the genre, counting back to Cindy Campbell's house party. The first public, or at least televised, celebration was February 5, 2023, at the Grammy Awards, seven days before Dave's passing. Ahmir "Questlove" Thompson of the Roots organized a fifteen-minute roller-coaster ride through the genre's history, from Grandmaster Flash and the Furious Five to Lil Uzi Vert. Each artist had thirty seconds or less to perform one of their classic songs.

Somewhere in the middle of the segment, soon after Public Enemy left the stage—at just about the right time chronologically—the backdrop turned to bright, fluorescent flowers and Posdnuos emerged in front of them, performing about twenty seconds of De La Soul's "Buddy" before passing the mic to Scarface. It was a meaningful inclusion for a group that was getting ready to emerge from a state of semi-invisibility. Both Dave and Maseo missed the event for health reasons. Before that was public knowledge, theirs was a glaring absence for such a long-running unit.

How many musical trios can you think of that stuck together for over thirty years with no public breakups or squabbles? Take the odds against that type of longevity, and add to them the risk factors of youth, the newness of their genre, and the historical inequities of the music industry— the sheer number of young Black artists taken advantage of by corporations, across genre and era.

In that light, De La Soul has carried the aura of an indestructible force bonded by friendship, creative freedom, eccentricity, and loyalty. It started with kids in school finding common ground in their exploration of a still-new musical art form, so new that at first it wasn't even thought of as a genre. They navigated overnight success, high-profile lawsuits, industry shenanigans, media stereotyping, the grind of exhaustive touring, and many other challenges. They grew De La Soul into a rock-solid partnership with a unique artistic legacy.

Even after Dave's passing, De La Soul lives on. Since that event in March 2023, the duo has been on an ongoing celebratory/memorial tour. In 2023 alone, even amid the shock of tragedy, De La Soul played Coachella with Gorillaz, toured with Wu-Tang Clan & Nas on the NY State of Mind tour, collaborated with Robert Glasper at the Blue Note Jazz Festival of Napa Valley, performed at some dates on the commemorative F.O.R.C.E. tour, and handled publicity around the rerelease of their music.

In the Yahoo interview, Maseo declared, "Every member has to actually die before this thing can be over." Posdnuos rhymed something similar in 2004 on the song "Rock Co.Kane Flow": "We De La to the death or at least until we break up."

In the *Beat Street* memorial scene, a photo of Ramo shows him standing next to a graffiti piece with the words: "It's Bigger than Me, I Just Can't Stop." That sentiment is reminiscent of the work ethic driving De La Soul to continue, for over thirty years and onward into the future, even after tragedy and struggle. It brings to mind the continuum of Black creativity that led to De La Soul, from the records in their parents' collections through to the earliest experimenters that spawned hip-hop culture and music.

The story of De La Soul is bigger than the trio themselves, even if you look just at the music. Their approach was rooted in collaboration at every step of the way: their dialogue with the ghosts of past artists and performers through sampling, their working partnerships with like-minded musicians. The community those collaborations created opened up new possibilities within the genre and beyond.

Their story is about loyalty as an overriding principle, creativity as the foundation for friendship (or vice versa), and resilience within the roller coaster that is the music industry. It is the story of a drive to keep something good going until the last possible moment.

I come to this story as one small speck within a galaxy that expands outward in many directions. I turned fifty the same month that hip-hop did. I grew up in the near-suburbs of St. Louis, Missouri, and am one of the white listeners who learned about the music after it was commercialized enough to reach me, via the channels of radio, MTV, and word of mouth. I borrowed LL Cool J and Run-D.M.C. tapes from elementary school classmates. I watched *Yo! MTV Raps* with host Fab 5 Freddy every Saturday morning, recorded it, and rewatched it. On Friday nights I listened to a rap radio show (*African Alert*, KDHX) when my classmates were at sporting events. I would ride my bike to one of two record stores (one for new, the other for used) to buy rap cassettes. I was one of the teenagers whose parents *Newsweek* was trying to scare with its 1990 cover story "Rap Rage," which declared, on the cover, "Yo! Street rhyme has gone big time. But are those sounds out of bounds?"

"Why do white people like De La Soul so much?" a Black co-worker at my summer job asked me in 1990. Ice Cube was her favorite. I don't think I had a good answer. This book will point toward a few: the way the group was marketed by their record label, the music they sampled, their suburban background, the way the "concept album" construction inadvertently plays into the hand of rock listeners used to thinking about albums in that way.

What first struck me was the lo-fi "Potholes in My Lawn" video, where they seemed to be just hanging out and speaking in code. At that time, I was eagerly soaking up rap music of all types, but De La Soul's eclectic sampling and off-kilter personalities especially resonated with me, a kid who through radio listening, tape collecting, and library checkouts was trying to hear it all, the history of music, and get beneath its surface.

De La Soul's *3 Feet High and Rising* contained a music history lesson, or at least a time-traveling tour, built into it. Its aesthetic echoed with other childhood interests, comic books and role-playing games. But I never thought of the music as sixties-ish, or De La Soul as "hippies." They seemed as much a part of hip-hop culture as Eric B. & Rakim, MC Lyte, Boogie Down Productions, or any of the other artists I was fascinated with, who each brought their own style.

There are numerous books lying in wait within the story of De La Soul, including how-to lessons in agility, perseverance, innovation, and problem-solving. Their story connects with the stories of many other hip-hop artists, movements, and events—some of which will be partially told here. Above all, this is a book about how young creatives managed to build their fascination into fun, their fun into art, and their art into a professional career that built a legacy for the ages.

2. DIFFERENT, BUT DOPE: YOUTH CULTURE AND THE MEMBERS OF DE LA SOUL

Though he considered the film watered down, *Beat Street* had its roots in Steve Hager's reporting for the *Village Voice* about early hip-hop groups in the Bronx. His 1982 article "Looking for the Perfect Beat" was named after a song from the same year by Afrika Bambaataa & Soulsonic Force. "A bunch of high school kids making up their own culture" is how Hager described the scene in a *Beat Street* oral history published in 2014 by eMusic's online publication *Wondering Sound*. A decade after what we now consider the birth date of the genre, the early eighties was a time when hip-hop had become the dominant means of self-expression for urban youth in the greater New York City region. Kids were rapping in the lunchroom, breakdancing in their driveways, and forming impromptu parties in parks and other neighborhood gathering places. It wasn't just a musical genre being born; it was an active youth culture.

The same kids rhyming on the school bus or breaking in the parks were sneaking late-night listens to the few NYC radio DJs that played rap music, 9:00 p.m. and after. The radio DJs didn't just play the music, they were integral to its creation, as John Klaess describes in his 2022 book *Breaks in the Air: The Birth of Rap Radio in New York City*. In radio studios, DJs such as John "Mr. Magic" Rivas at WBLS and Frederick Crute, a.k.a. Kool DJ Red Alert, at KISS-FM, were experimenting in their own right. Rap radio DJs attempted to channel the music of the streets into a show format. It was a precursor to the sample-heavy direction the musical genre would head.

De La Soul would be spawned, in part, from this overall culture that had become ubiquitous not just in the boroughs that birthed hip-hop and the surrounding areas, but in metro areas across the US that looked toward NYC as the heartbeat of youth culture. In his 2019 memoir *Sweat the Technique*, the rapper Rakim calls hip-hop in the late seventies and early eighties, "already a lot more than just a sound . . . it was a whole experience."

The members of De La Soul were the younger brothers and nephews of hip-hop, the first generation after the founders. Each had roots in one of the five boroughs, and moved to Long Island in their youth. They had relatives back in Brooklyn, Queens, or the Bronx, connecting them back to the source. Long Island was the playground for kids who were exposed to the hip-hop culture of the city but had the freedom of space that came with living in the suburbs. De La Soul's families are among those that moved out of the city to give their children a better life.

Paul Huston, a.k.a. Prince Paul, told the *Crate 808* podcast that the suburbs make people think, "Grass, trees, there's really no hip-hop in that." Yet the movement of Black families from each of the boroughs to Long Island made for a consolidation, "essentially, the five boroughs piled into one."

In the 2023 *New York Times* feature "50 Rappers, 50

Stories," for the fiftieth anniversary of hip-hop, LL Cool accentuated this point. Though always repping Queens, LL relayed that he learned more about hip-hop when he was living in Long Island, because he lived next door to a house where foster kids from all five boroughs lived. They'd bring tapes directly back from each borough. "I was hearing everything way earlier. I was hearing it as it was unfolding."

In the *Village Voice* in 1991, Nelson George described Long Island's best-known rappers—Public Enemy, EPMD, Eric B. & Rakim—as coming from "home-owning, civil service-job-working, Black middle-class environments." He wrote that you can hear that background most within De La Soul's music. There is a freedom and diversity that the group themselves relate to their roots; to them being of the city and also outside of it. De La Soul have explained in interviews that Long Island gave them the space to try different things, even use music that might feel more at odds with their surroundings had they lived in the projects.

Vincent Mason Jr., a.k.a. DJ Maseo or P.A. Pasemaster Mase, was the youngest of the three founding members of De La Soul, but he may have been exposed to hip-hop the earliest. He was born in 1970 and grew up in Brooklyn, raised by his mom during the earliest years of hip-hop culture. He was fascinated by the music and what was going on around it. His earliest memories include witnessing block parties and DJs performing in the park.

He learned about hip-hop from cousins, uncles, and his sister's boyfriend. The first person to let him play around with DJ equipment was a man named Rick, dating a girl who he thought of as an older sister. He let Mase try out scratching on a batch of funk and disco records popular with party DJs at the time: "Good Times" by Chic, "Super

Sperm" by Captain Sky, "Catch a Groove" by Juice, "Frisco Disco" by Eastside Connection.

Mase had his own first set of turntables in 1976, early Technics, which would later be a standard brand for DJs. This was more of a starter model; he still needed to use a coin to balance the cartridge. Having his own set let him mess around with records at home, on his own, at age six. Soon he would carry records and equipment for the neighborhood DJs, helping them get set up for parties. This gave him a closer view of what the DJs were doing. In 1979 he got his first DJ mixer, a Spearsonic with an up/down fader that his uncle helped him connect with two record players broken out from component systems. He learned to blend beats by using greasy wax paper from Chinese-restaurant fried chicken as a slipmat.

In 1982, when he was twelve, he DJed his mom's housewarming party. It was an all-night event that he later cited as the best gig he ever played. That same year he was the DJ at a block party for the first time, in Bushwick, Brooklyn. He met local figures involved in the music industry, older neighbors like singers Stephanie Mills and Gwen Guthrie. It was a year that felt like the start of something. It was his "induction into hip-hop," as he told Red Bull Music Academy (RBMA) in a 2012 video interview.

He started wanting to make a record of his own. The biggest spark was hearing the 1984 single "It's Yours" by T La Rock, with scratches by Jazzy Jay of Soulsonic Force over a beat that Rick Rubin made in his NYU dorm on a Roland TR-808 drum machine. It was the first time Mase heard a rapper over a drum break within the format of a song. "That's when I said, Yo, I really wanna do this . . . that was *it* for me," he told interviewer Damien "Lil D" Morgan in 2005.

Mason and his mother moved to Amityville, Long Island, in 1984, when he was fourteen. He immediately became a part of the scene, DJing at parties and meeting local hip-hop heads. It was a competitive environment with rappers and groups performing at parties, civic festivals, and competitions. Rakim, then known as Kid Wizard (a.k.a. Love Kid Wiz), was performing as part of the Love Brothers. Freddie Foxxx was part of Supreme Force. Biz Markie (then Bizzy B Markie), from the more rural east side of Long Island, was frequently around.

In 1985, Mason DJed a party where he made $300, his first payment for DJing. "I felt like I was in the business," he told RBMA. He'd see Kool G Rap in the audience sometimes when he DJed, or Prince Markie Dee of the Fat Boys. When Mase moved to Long Island, he thought he was getting farther away from his dream of making hip-hop records, but now he was getting closer to it, becoming part of something.

One of the groups roaming Amityville Memorial Junior High, playing at parties and events, around 1984, was Easy Street: three rappers, a DJ, and a "human beatbox." They were five kids from the neighborhood trying to make music together. The human beatbox was Dave Jolicoeur, going by his middle name, Jude. Kelvin Mercer was the DJ, known as DJ Sop Sound. He had proposed Sop Sounds as the group name, but they didn't like it; they preferred Easy Street, so he kept it as his DJ name instead. Mercer has explained Sop Sound in numerous interviews with a personal memory. His mom was from Georgia and she would tell him to sop up everything on his plate with a piece of bread. A DJ similarly sops up all the sounds around him.

Mercer had moved from the Bronx to Long Island

the year before. One of the first friends he made was his elementary school classmate Mike Jolicoeur, Dave's younger brother. The Jolicoeurs, whose parents were of Haitian descent, had moved from Brooklyn to East Massapequa, Long Island.

Kelvin Mercer and Dave Jolicoeur were fast friends, and developed their own style of speaking, dressing, and goofing around. They were popular, social kids who invented their own language so no one knew what they were saying, and created unique outfits to wear. They would take their fathers' plaid pants and sew them to be pulled up high. Jolicoeur would cut designs into his hair. They started rapping together in Mercer's basement, at ages eleven and twelve.

They didn't rap publicly yet, but they wrote many of the rhymes for the three rappers in Easy Street. The rest of Easy Street weren't on the same page, musically, as Mercer and Jolicoeur, so the two of them split from the group and kept working on music together. Jude and DJ Sop Sound were imitating the strangeness of the Ultramagnetic MCs, a NYC-based group whose MCs, especially Kool Keith, trafficked in a word-dense style with unlikely turns of phrase. In a 1989 *New Musical Express* interview with Paolo Hewitt, Jolicoeur said the Easy Street rappers were more used to basic rhyme styles: "they couldn't really adapt to what we were writing."

After Easy Street dissolved, Mercer and Jolicoeur teamed up with a schoolmate who DJed: Charles F. Smith Jr., known then as DJ Charlie Rock (later as DJ Stitches). Smith had played basketball with Mike Jolicoeur, who told him about his brother's unique style of rapping: "it's different, but it's dope." Mercer told *A.V. Club* in 2000 that when Charlie Rock joined up with him and Dave, it was the turning point in them deciding to rhyme, and they let Charlie handle the DJing.

Smith had moved to North Amityville, Long Island, when he was in ninth grade, after growing up in Queens. The next year, Vincent Mason and Charles Smith met and started a DJ crew together called Mack Productions. In an interview with Red Bull Music Academy, Mase said they thought of themselves like Chill Will and Barry B, the two DJs supporting Doug E. Fresh & the Get Fresh Crew. Those two separate collaborations—Mercer, Jolicoeur, and Smith becoming a group of sorts, and Mason and Smith forming a DJ crew—would soon unite into one. Charlie Rock "was actually the person who brought us all together," Mase said.

What would become De La Soul was at first just four friends hanging out and messing around with music. They'd try to impress each other with the coolest or most interesting combinations of sounds. Each of them would share musical ideas, pulling samples from records as a foundation for songs. One would bring an idea and the others would add to it.

Any LP they got their hands on was a potential source to pull from. The record collections of their parents and siblings were the key building blocks for their creative output. They would search through the collections of their friends' parents and grandparents, looking for music they could mine for ideas.

In the summer of 1985, they hung out nearly every day in their basements and bedrooms to mess around with sounds from their parents' records and try out the burgeoning science of hip hop, through the most rudimentary means. They were in summer school together, and would take any opportunity to cut out early, go across the street to Mase's house and mess around with music. They've described having an immediate chemistry. Hours would fly by. Mase's mom would bring them juice and cookies while they worked on music.

"There wasn't a blueprint," Mason told *Classic Pop Magazine* in 2022. One of them would have an idea that another one liked, and they would follow it where it took them. "We'd hang around working on that idea for the day or the week." No one knew Mercer and Jolicoeur rapped, so their musical playing-around carried an air of secrecy. Mason and Smith kept their friends' secret for close to two years.

Without any plan for what they were working toward, they'd take records, sample them in rudimentary ways, and build them into something they could record. Mercer had a Casio SK-1 keyboard that had preprogrammed sounds, plus four sample pads with which you could record short segments of sound, four seconds at a time. They would put the keyboard up against the speaker of their stereo system, record the "sample" of the record they were playing onto the keyboard, and then play it back, recording the playback on their cassette deck. Mase had a Dr. Rhythm drum machine for creating the beats. Before they got a four-track tape recorder, they would use a double cassette deck to record and overdub. To make a loop, they'd record the "sample" onto the other tape, pause, rewind it, and record again. This would link together the sample into a loop, making what are referred to as pause tapes. To do this, they borrowed equipment from friends and relatives.

They worked on some songs that would eventually be on their debut album: "The Magic Number," "Ghetto Thang," "D.A.I.S.Y. Age," and "Potholes in My Lawn." The songs didn't have those names yet and, at this point, they didn't have a name for the group. They performed live once, at the high school talent show (they did what later became "Ghetto Thang"), but otherwise kept the music to themselves. It was a private creative endeavor, with no plan.

The other person important to the birth of De La Soul—an unofficial but integral member—is Paul Huston, a.k.a. DJ Paul and later Prince Paul. Mase considers Paul to be "the dude that made it happen," as he told 247HH.com in 2018. When Huston joined the fray, they put together all the pieces that became De La Soul.

Three years older than Mason, Huston was similarly obsessed with music from a young age. In a 1999 oral history of Prince Paul's career in *The Source*, his mother, Peggy Huston, recalled having to put a boom box in his baby carriage to keep him happy. He had a Mickey Mouse turntable and began collecting records when he was five. The collecting was influenced by his older siblings who were teenagers and had their own turntables and records, and by his dad, who loved jazz. Huston has told interviewers the first two records he owned were the 45 rpm singles of James Brown's "Hot Pants" and King Floyd's "Groove Me." "Even before toys, I was listening," he told the *Serato Unscripted* podcast in 2022.

He learned about hip-hop from seeing parties in parks in Long Island and Brooklyn. This was before DJs were scratching records; they played disco breaks at parties. Huston was born in Queens and moved to Long Island when he was four or five, but he would also visit his grandmother in Brooklyn, bringing what he learned about hip-hop back to Long Island.

Huston started DJing in 1977, when he was ten. He spent hours at home messing around with record players, trying to figure them out. He took an old stereo receiver, put one turntable broken out from a stereo component set on the left side and another similar turntable on the right. He connected them through the console, set it to mono, and then used the balance knob, which controlled the balance between the left and right speakers, as a mixer. He told *The Source* in 1999, "I was like the MacGyver of hip-hop!"

He tried to learn all the DJ tricks and do them better than anyone else. He scratched records behind his back, under his leg, and using his mouth—the type of moves that would later be described as "turntablism." Under the name DJ Paul, he participated in battles where everyone showed off their skills. He thought he was the best in the world; kids in the neighborhood would call him "Fake Grandmaster Flash." When DJing, he told *Wax Poetics* magazine in 2002, he would sometimes throw in "weird stuff just to bug people out."

Huston would ride his bike around the neighborhood, hear the "thump thump" of music, and navigate to parties in backyards or parks. He'd position himself by the DJ and watch while everyone else danced. He wanted to understand what they were doing, figure out their maneuvers and what specific records they were using. He gained an early knowledge of the most common breakbeats when he realized that even though DJs would wash off the labels so their competitors didn't see the records, they would put those LPs back in their original jackets after they played them. After figuring out the records, he'd go buy them himself when he got money for his birthday.

When he was eleven or twelve, neighbors who rhymed asked him to be their DJ. The group was called the Everready Crew, so he took the name DJ Everready and had a shirt with that name across it. In eighth grade he DJed for Bizzy B, a.k.a. Biz Markie. Biz, three years older, was an always-roaming Long Island character who would beatbox at parties and show up at schools to publicize his shows. Biz was so likable the principal at Amityville Memorial High would let him come into the school and just hang around. Dave told the *Juan Ep Is Life* podcast in 2015: "Biz used to hang out in the cafeteria all day." Biz and Paul would make tapes together, with Biz putting rhymes he had written over known breakbeats that Paul had heard at the park.

When he was finishing the eleventh grade, around age sixteen, Huston joined Stetsasonic as their DJ. The Brooklyn-based Stetsasonic started as a high school group back in 1981, formed by friends Glenn Bolton, a.k.a. Daddy-O, and Marvin Shahid Wright, a.k.a. MC Delite. In 1984 they won a record-label deal for a single, as the prize for a Mr. Magic–hosted cross-borough rap contest. "We won hands down against everybody," Daddy-O told 247HH. They signed with Tommy Boy Records after getting an offer from Sugar Hill that they thought was horrible.

Tommy Boy would play a big role in the future of Stetsasonic, Prince Paul, and ultimately De La Soul. The label had stature at the time, one of a few independent labels started by white men drawn to the emerging hip-hop culture. Tom Silverman started the label as an outgrowth of his music newsletter, *Dance Music Report*. The origins of the label go back to a time Silverman was browsing for records at Downstairs Records, in Midtown Manhattan. He kept seeing kids go into a back room and come out with records. It was the store's "B-Boy Room," where they kept the breakbeat records. A 1978 *Billboard* article "B-Beats Bombarding Bronx," by Robert Ford Jr., takes note of this same phenomenon, starting, "A funny thing has been happening at Downstairs Records . . ."

The kids tell Silverman they learned about the breakbeats from Afrika Bambaataa. He starts going to see Bambaataa deejay at T-Connection in the Bronx, offers to put out a record, and brings in dance producer Arthur Baker to oversee it. "Jazzy Sensation" sold 35,000 copies out of Silverman's apartment. The next single, "Planet Rock," became an even bigger crossover success, selling 650,000 records and drawing interest overseas. The first hip-hop record with global reach, its success came less than a year after Tommy Boy was started. At that point it turned from a twelve-inch dance label into a proper record company, signing acts and releasing albums.

In December 1981, Tom Silverman hired the first Tommy Boy employee, who would later be important to De La Soul's success. Monica Lynch, twenty-five years old, had moved to New York City from Chicago to be a model. She ended up working as a bartender, an actress, an assistant to a fashion designer, a member of a punk band, and a go-go dancer. She responded to a Tommy Boy help wanted ad and started multi-tasking at the label. She worked with the distributors and artists, handled paperwork and promotion. She even wrote a column in issues of Silverman's *Dance Music Report*. She did "anything and everything you can possibly imagine," she told Jeff "Chairman" Mao on the *Across 135th Street* podcast.

In just a few years Monica Lynch would become president of Tommy Boy. She would go on to help the label navigate a series of challenging years, all well documented in Dan Charnas's 2010 book *The Big Payback: The History of the Business of Hip-Hop*. Charnas writes that Tommy Boy "set the archetype for independent prowess." Warner

Bros. purchased half the label in 1985, while still giving the company the choice of distributing albums independently or through the major label.

After signing to Tommy Boy in 1984, Stetsasonic needed a DJ, and they knew about DJ Paul. The pivotal moment came at a DJ battle at the Brevoort Day Celebration, at the Brevoort Projects in Bed-Stuy, Brooklyn. "All the big deejays used to be out there," Daddy-O told interviewer Ryan Proctor in 2013. Paul decided to go with neighbors at the last minute. During the battle, Stetsasonic watched Paul doing a routine with the Liquid Liquid song "Cavern," taking the cymbal from the beginning and playing it back and forth. They approached Paul after his set. They were wearing black leather and Daddy-O had a spiked dog collar; "*Beat Street*–style clothes" is how Paul described their outfits to *The Source*. He thought they were going to beat him up. Instead, they asked him to join the group, and he agreed.

Since Huston was only sixteen years old, Stetsasonic came to his house to talk to his family and get their approval. He worked with Stetsasonic on the demo for their first single, "Just Say Stet," and continued with them from there. Huston told *Pitchfork*, "I didn't even know what a demo was back then. I didn't know what a studio was, either—I was a kid!" He would make tapes of beats and mail them to Daddy-O, and Daddy-O would write letters back in response. For his contributions to Stetsasonic's debut album *On Fire*, Prince Paul was paid $600. He used some of the money to buy a VCR from department store JCPenney, so he could mix his music in stereo.

From Prince Paul's perspective, Stetsasonic was Daddy-O's group. Paul knew he'd have limited creative control. Even when he did contribute, he wouldn't always get credit.

Prince Paul and Frukwan programmed the beat for "Sally" and went uncredited. For "Talkin' All That Jazz," Prince Paul brought in his friend Don Newkirk to play an instrumental part that Daddy-O was struggling to sample from Lonnie Liston Smith's "Expansions." On the record, the only credits are for MC Delite as producer and Daddy-O as co-producer.

In the studio, if Prince Paul went to touch the buttons, his hand would be swatted away. When he'd bring tracks he was working on, Daddy-O would tell him they were too weird for Stetsasonic. Daddy-O has confirmed this is how Prince Paul's ideas were handled. He told Ryan Proctor, "I thought that Paul had a bunch of silly things that he wanted to do." Stetsasonic songs that Paul did influence, according to Daddy-O, are the interludes "Your Mother Has Green Teeth" and "Paul's a Sucker," and the song "Music for the Stetfully Insane," which samples Funkadelic and an *Amazing Spider-Man* record.

Prince Paul and Vincent Mason knew each other from the local scene. But the important day that brought them together, in 1987, involved Everett Collins, the music teacher at Amityville Memorial High and Junior High. Collins lived down the street from the Mercers and was a high school friend of Vincent Mason's mom. A drummer and the son of a drummer, Collins had played with the Isley Brothers and was a founding member of the groups Sunrize and Surface (their song "Happy" hit #2 on the *Billboard* R&B chart in 1987). He had a record label of his own, Alexadon Records, named after his daughters. He signed a local rapper named Gangster "B," Eric Riley, to the label. Riley was the best friend of Mase's uncle and a classmate of Prince Paul. "He had this style that was almost like Run, of Run-D.M.C.," Mason told *Serato Unscripted*.

Mase did some DJing for Gangster "B" and was invited to a recording studio to add scratches in a session that led to the single "Cold Waxin' the Party." Prince Paul was invited as well to produce beats, using his Sequential Tom drum machine. What they were working on was "really, really, really wack," Mase told Red Bull Music Academy. Prince Paul was asked to do a backward beat like the Beastie Boys used in "Paul Revere," something he didn't feel comfortable with, because he felt like he'd be "biting" someone else's style. During breaks in the session, Mase and Paul bonded over their discontent with the music and talked about their own musical plans.

A few days after the session, Prince Paul stopped by the school to find Mase, to play him some music. He approached Mase near the cafeteria, and Mase cut school for the rest of the day so they could listen to music together. In Prince Paul's car he played Mase some of the tracks for Stetsasonic's second album, *In Full Gear*, plus tracks he had created that Daddy-O rejected. "It was incredible stuff," Mase told 247HH, "so in the lane of what we were working on."

They went to Mase's house, and he in turn played Paul the music he'd been working on with Jolicoeur and Mercer. He played him early versions of "Plug Tunin'," "Potholes in My Lawn," "Freedom of Speak," "The Magic Number" (which didn't have a title yet), "De La Game" (which became "D.A.I.S.Y. Age"), and a track that would much later become part of the intro to the *Stakes Is High* album.

Both Mase and Paul recognized something in the other's music that felt familiar. They had a similar approach to sampling and music in general. Mase left Prince Paul with the tape of "Plug Tunin'" and said he'd be back the next day. Meanwhile, Prince Paul started adding things to the song, overdubbing onto additional cassettes.

Prince Paul made his additions and then used the VCR he bought with the Stetsasonic money to make a "master mix" of "Plug Tunin'" on a VHS tape, his only way to achieve stereo sound. When Mase returned to hear the results, he brought Mercer and Jolicoeur along. Prince Paul described his first impression on Open Mike Eagle's *What Had Happened Was* podcast in 2020: "These guys rhyme? They're nerdier than me . . . and I'm a big nerd."

This was the start of the next stage in De La Soul's evolution: Prince Paul working with the others to build off what they'd started, helping them get a demo in shape to shop around to labels. "Prince Paul didn't make any promises," Mase explained to interviewer DJ Frenic in 2016, but told them, "We're going to take this stuff to a studio and clean it up."

Prince Paul worked with the group to help define their sound. "Our sounds and our ideas fitted so perfectly," he said in the oral history book *The Hip Hop Years*. He would sometimes bring them specific music elements to add to their songs, and sometimes just make a suggestion that they could explore together. They listened to him. In Brian Coleman's book *Check the Technique: Liner Notes for Hip-Hop Junkies*, Dave recalled, "Paul could really stretch records out. We'd let him add just one more thing, and it was always the cherry on top. There was never a time when Paul didn't make a song better, where he didn't find exactly what was missing."

The group was named around the time they were pursuing a record deal, either soon before Prince Paul was part of it, or soon after. Mercer proposed the name From the Soul. "I just felt that everything we try to do will be from the soul," he said in *The Hip Hop Years*. Dave thought it was a cool idea but sounded corny, so he suggested De La Soul. The idea came from Dave's interest in foreign languages. (Both Daddy-O and Wise of Stetsasonic have suggested De La's name was inspired by another source: the 1986 Stetsasonic song "Rock De La Stet.") In the early days, the name brought some confusion. People who had only heard the name thought they played Latin music.

Somewhere in the process of their transition to becoming De La Soul as we know it, Charlie Rock dropped out of the picture. Whether it was because of his own demeanor/behavior within the group, or he and Prince Paul not getting along, or the record label not wanting a group with two DJs because they already had Too Poetic (the trio from Wyandanch, Long Island, of rapper Poetic and DJs Kaos and Woody Wood), or a combination of all that, is hard to tell.

The details of his contributions to the early recordings are unclear; it's something the group doesn't talk much about. Smith has said "Plug Tunin'" was recorded at his mom's house, that he chose some of their most famous samples, and that he helped Dave come up with the group's "bug-out pieces" (skits). His nephew, the underground rapper/producer Elucid, has described it as an often-told family story he heard growing up, that De La Soul's demo was recorded at his grandmother's house. Smith told Unkut.com he should be considered the original member of De La because he brought them all together. "The rest of them are Plugs Two, Three and Four—I'm Plug fuckin' One."

Charlie Rock left before De La Soul had a name, and before they signed a record deal. "When it all came together, he was out of the picture," Mase told Lil D in 2005. Dave told the *Juan Ep* podcast in 2015, "He basically didn't fit the whole vibe, and he wanted to do his own thing as well." In a 2014 interview with Unkut.com, Charlie Rock himself told a more bitter version of the story: "They had a secret meeting, voted me out of the group and took the deal."

3. BELIEVE WHAT WE BELIEVE: GETTING STARTED, GETTING SIGNED, AND THE FIRST SINGLES

De La Soul has mentioned various early groups they were influenced by: Run-D.M.C., Fat Boys, Boogie Down Productions, and the Treacherous Three. But their most frequently cited influence is the Ultramagnetic MCs, especially the unusual approach Kool Keith took to rhymes. Mase told Red Bull Music Academy in 2012, "That was the inspiration to be like, 'Yeah, we going to be different. We're going to come out with our own language. We going to make you believe what we believe.'"

Ultramagnetic MCs was formed by high school friends in the Bronx in 1984 as an extension of their lunchtime rhyming. At first it was Keith Thornton, a.k.a. Kool Keith; Cedric Miller, a.k.a. Ced-Gee; and Cedric's cousin Moe Love. The group's debut album, *Critical Beatdown*, with Ced-Gee as the primary producer, is seen as a crucial step forward in the development of sampling. In Brian Coleman's book *Rakim Told Me*, Prince Paul cited the 1986 Ultramagnetic MCs single "Ego Trippin'" as the first time he heard someone loop a beat: "I was like, Wow, you can *do* that??!"

Kool Keith was the most unconventional rapper of the

group, with psychological obsessions and a flair for using unexpected words. In 2021, he described his approach to interviewer David Ma as "always trying to say things that haven't been said before."

For De La Soul, a similar attitude was behind their lyrics and the very presentation of themselves as a group: their mutable stage names, their own slang. A De La Soul–curated issue of the quarterly hip-hop magazine *Frank151*, published in 2012, included "The Delacratic Dictionary," a brief glossary of phrases they created, such as Dan Stuckie ("dope or fresh") and black fog ("a fart").

Individually their first rap names, per a BBC1 Radio interview, were MC Logiticus (Mercer), Devious D (Jolicoeur), and Vince the Prince (Mason). By the time De La Soul came together, they had names that took their childhood roots and purported food preferences and twisted them into signs of the new language they were trying to create. Mason was going by P.A. Pasemaster Mase. That play on his birth name was also an ode to the sound system culture of early hip-hop. Mercer was Posdnuos, a reversal of his DJ name Sop Sound. Jolicoeur was Trugoy the Dove. Dove stemmed from his beatbox name JD Dove; Trugoy because at the time he ate a lot of yogurt.

They also were known as Plugs 1, 2, and 3, something that came about more organically. When they would perform in these early days, at neighborhood parties, their set consisted of stage routines inspired by groups like the Cold Crush Brothers and Crash Crew, over familiar breakbeat songs such as "Impeach the President" by the Honey Drippers. "Plug Tunin'" was one of those routines before it became a song. Mercer and Jolicoeur would do a call-and-response rhyme based on the idea of plugs: "Plug One?" "Plug Two."

"It was just a chant, almost like a count," Pos told the *Drink Champs* podcast in 2023, similar to an MC or singer starting with a microphone check like "One-two, one-two." Audience members interpreted those as the rappers' stage names. They'd call Mercer Plug 1 and Jolicoeur Plug 2. By default, Mason became known as Plug 3.

Prince Paul told *Wax Poetics* that De La told him the name came from when you plug a microphone into a speaker. But there's another connection. On some 45 singles sent to radio stations for promotion, the A-side would be listed as the "Plug Side," meaning the song the label wanted to be plugged, or promoted. That was true of the record they used for the most prominent sample, on "Plug Tunin'": "Written on the Wall" by the Invitations. It was a record Posdnuos pulled from his dad's collection of soul and doo-wop. The routine "Plug Tunin'" evolved into more of a song when they started using the "Written on the Wall" loop. From there, they'd keep tweaking the song in different directions. "It was a hundred different ways we did 'Plug Tunin'' before you guys really know it," Mase told 247HH.

At Prince Paul's encouragement, they took "Plug Tunin'" and "Freedom of Speak" to Calliope Studios, on Thirty-Seventh Street between Seventh and Eighth Avenues in Manhattan, to build them into a demo they could share. A place Stetsasonic and Biz Markie had recorded at before, Calliope would become a foundational studio for the early part of De La Soul's career.

During the Calliope sessions for the demo, initial singles, and then their debut album, De La Soul and Prince Paul would take the Long Island Rail Road to the studio in the afternoon, walking from Penn Station to the studio, carrying their records. Calliope resembled a loft apartment more than a studio. It was a comfortable place for the group to hang out and keep working on their songs. Chris Julian, who founded the studio in 1984, offered studio time at around half the price of the nearest competitor. At times, De La Soul and Prince Paul recorded there overnight, because it was even cheaper: thirty-five dollars an hour for studio time.

While translating the four-track version to a twenty-four-track version for the demo, Prince Paul added some touches to "Plug Tunin'" that built it up further (he made it "120 percent better than what we did," Posdnuos told Brian Coleman for *Check the Technique*). There's the piano part from Billy Joel's "Stiletto," a snippet of James Brown's "I'm Shook," and the breakbeat from "Midnight Theme" by Manzel, a Kentucky funk band from the late seventies. (The same beat would fuel Cypress Hill's "How I Could Just Kill a Man" a few years later.)

The demo included three songs: "Plug Tunin'," "Freedom of Speak," and "De La Game" (which later became "D.A.I.S.Y. Age"). Prince Paul used his connections to shop the demo around to labels, with help from Daddy-O of Stetsasonic. Daddy-O had two other artists whose demos he was sharing with labels. He told Prince Paul he was willing to help handle the De La Soul demo as well, even though he only liked "Plug Tunin'" and thought they sounded too much like Ultramagnetic. It likely surprised him when the labels were more interested in De La Soul than the artists he was trying to sell.

Prince Paul and De La Soul have said the demo was sent to every big indie hip-hop label of the moment, as well as some majors. The group received offers and interest from multiple labels. MC Lyte and Audio Two were trying to bring De La Soul their direction, to First Priority. Profile and Geffen both made offers to put out a single, for more money than Tommy Boy offered. Profile, founded by Cory Robbins in 1980, had been a big success, with Run-D.M.C. as their marquee artist. Geffen was trying to break into hip-hop but didn't have any acts yet. (In 1988 they would sign the 7A3 as their first, and then years later the Roots.)

Monica Lynch was the first to hear the demo at Tommy Boy. De La Soul also showed the label their notebook of ideas, to demonstrate the potential. She has recalled being instantly intrigued by both De La Soul the people and the music. "It sounded radically different from anything I'd ever heard," Lynch said in the oral history *The Come Up*. She often uses the word "dusted" to describe the vibe of what she heard. Tom Silverman has also described the demo as something truly different, so much so that he wasn't sure how successful it'd be. "It was either gonna be nothing or be gigantic," Silverman recalled in *The Hip Hop Years*.

They signed within a few days of Tommy Boy receiving the tape. Reportedly, the demo reached Monica Lynch on a Friday, and by Monday they had a completed deal. Prince Paul was the lone voice of dissent. Based on his experience with Tommy Boy while in Stetsasonic, especially what he saw as their lack of financial support for music videos and other promotion, he wanted the group to sign with Profile or with Geffen, the label offering the largest sum of money.

De La Soul felt most comfortable with Monica Lynch and Tommy Boy. Posdnuos told *Ebony* in 2016 that Monica Lynch herself was a big part of what drew them to sign with the label: she "had a genuine inner-good; her energy was electric." They also felt some comfort knowing that Prince Paul had been working with the label already.

Prince Paul has said that Daddy-O gets undue credit

for connecting De La Soul to Tommy Boy Records. Rodd Houston, who worked at Tommy Boy and happened to be in the studio when they were working on the demo, is the one who encouraged Prince Paul and Daddy-O to go to Tommy Boy with the De La Soul demo.

Upon signing, De La Soul quickly fell in with the hip-hop scene of the moment, hanging out at the rap parties and clubs, where they'd meet the hot rappers of the day. The Latin Quarter, near Times Square, was where groups like Stetsasonic and Jungle Brothers played and developed their live shows. Founded by Claude "Paradise" Gray and Lumumba Carson (Professor X of the group X Clan, son of activist Sonny Carson), it was the place for rappers and other scenesters of the moment to hang out, meet each other, and make deals.

New music broke through at clubs like the Latin Quarter. In an online article about the NYC club Building, DJ Stretch Armstrong described the synchronicity among radio and the club scene in that period: "You would go to a club, to hear records that were hot, but you're also going to hear new music. And that wasn't something that would frustrate people—that was something that people looked forward to."

Dante Ross was a twentysomething out on the town and at the hip-hop clubs every night. "I met the who's who of rap stars" at the Latin Quarter, he wrote in his 2023 memoir *Son of the City*. On the town is where he met Monica Lynch, through Daddy-O. She invited him in to interview for a job at Tommy Boy. He was hired to be their first official A&R representative, and his first project was helping promote De La Soul. At his first Tommy Boy office visit, Ross heard the De La Soul demo. He liked it. It was "the weirdest, coolest thing I ever heard," he wrote in *Son of the City*, also acknowledging that he didn't understand their style of dress ("way out, even by my downtown standards"). He was paid $28,000 a year, low enough that he still bartended, and sold weed out of his Tommy Boy office, to get by.

The group's first twelve-inch single was essentially the demo. "Plug Tunin' (Are You Ready for This?)" is set up as an introduction to De La Soul's approach to sampling and their unique rhyme styles. It starts with Mase speaking: "Yo, Pos and Dove, stand clear to be plugged up into line one and two so y'all can flaunt that new style of speak," with a sample of an official-sounding voice cutting in to say, "Good luck to both of you." The voice resembles Ground Control to astronauts, giving Mase's literal instructions a more otherworldly feeling that carries through the whole song.

The song has Posdnuos and J.D. Dove bragging about their abilities within a cloak of words ("prerogative praised positively, I'm acquitted"), introducing new terms for emcees ("paragraph preacher") and rhymes ("vocal confetti"), and alluding to the coming D.A.I.S.Y. Age. It feels abstract, fresh, and strange, yet at a base level the song is also quite literal. They're rhyming over music about the act of rhyming over music. Dove in the second verse gets biological about it: "Words are sent to the vents of humans / then converted to a phrase called talk." The voices of the obscure sixties soul group the Invitations ebb and flow across the track, echoing the fact that voice itself is the song's primary subject. The "Written on the Wall" sample was not well-known. Tommy Boy ran a contest offering $500 to anyone who could identify the sample, and no one won.

The twelve-inch also had "Freedom of Speak (We Got Three Minutes)" on the A-side, with additional versions of both "Plug" and "Freedom" on Side B, along with the thirty-eight-second "Strictly Dan Stuckie," the first example of what would become the group's trademark skits.

"Freedom of Speak" has a meta quality, with Prince Paul's voice telling them they have three minutes to rhyme ("to speak as free as possible") and then cutting them off when they hit the time limit. In the song, speaking freely means chronicling everyday actions—waking up, looking at the clock, taking a shower, turning on the news, and pondering why the world is so messed up—while ending every line of a verse with the same rhyming sound.

After its release in April 1988, "Plug Tunin'" took off quickly with local radio and at clubs. Dante Ross has claimed he walked the single to DJ Red Alert as soon as he had it in his hands, and Red Alert played it that night. That might have happened at a club (Red Alert regularly DJed at Latin Quarter), but on radio DJ Red Alert was not one of the first DJs to play it, per De La Soul's interview with Peter Rosenberg on the *Juan Ep* podcast. The first DJs to play the song were on college radio.

First was P Fine (a.k.a. Jonathan Finegold) on WNYU-FM. Pos specifically mentions him on "Freedom of Speak": "It was Tuesday / I had to tape P Fine." Second was André Brown, a.k.a. Doctor Dré of the group Original Concept, and later host of the weekday afternoon version of *Yo! MTV Raps*. Brown hosted a show on WBAU, the Adelphi University station where Chuck D, Bill Stephney, and MC DJ Flavor (later Flavor Flav) of Public Enemy had shows. Jeff Foss was third to play it, on WRHU from Hofstra University.

DJ Red Alert playing "Plug Tunin'" came later, but it was meaningful to the group. DJ Red Alert (Frederick Crute) was one of the hottest hip-hop DJs in NYC at the time. He was affiliated with Afrika Bambaataa's Zulu Nation, and he played a role in many of the notable rap events of the period, including the Boogie Down Productions / Juice Crew feud over the birthplace of hip-hop. Songs he played on KISS-FM, or at clubs, were almost guaranteed to be hits.

The first time he heard "Plug Tunin'" on the radio, David Jolicoeur was in a college dorm room. He was planning to study architecture and didn't yet realize how quickly his plans would change. Hearing it on the radio felt like complete success, reaching the biggest goal the group had envisioned for themselves. To hear their song played by DJs that they respected, and that they knew had the overall respect of the community, validated their creative direction.

The "Plug Tunin'" momentum built quickly over the late spring and early summer of 1988. All the local hip-hop radio shows were playing it, it was a hit in the clubs, and the group would hear from their label that it was starting to get played in other places across the country.

De La Soul's first official live performance was at Irving Plaza, on Irving Place near Union Square in Manhattan. Stetsasonic was celebrating the release of *In Full Gear*, as part of a weekly party called Payday (after the candy bar), which moved around downtown venues like the Ukrainian Hall, the Columns, the Cooperative Auditorium, and more, with house and hip-hop DJs performing. Tommy Boy booked De La to open the show.

Dante Ross wrote a piece for the De La Soul–curated *Frank151* issue, giving his chronicle of the night. In his retelling, Stetsasonic was fighting with Tommy Boy and didn't show up for their own release party. That left just De La Soul to perform. They had never performed a proper show to an audience and only had one full song ready. Their friend Granny introduced them. De La Soul performed a bit of "Freedom of Speak" and then "Plug Tunin'" with their dancers China and Jette holding up cue cards (which Dave had illustrated) in sync with the words of the song.

The crowd was enthusiastic. Dante Ross recalled, "I always remembered how hard they rocked it and how proud I was of them." Pos has described in various interviews that D.M.C. of Run-D.M.C. was right by the stage during their performance and kept yelling, "Do it again!" They told the *Juan Ep* podcast that Russell Simmons came over and told them, "I'm on your dick! I want to sign you."

In 1984, along with co-creating Def Jam Records, Simmons had started Rush Artist Management, offering management and publicity services to both Def Jam artists and artists on other labels. Music executive Lyor Cohen got his start in the industry managing artists as part of Rush.

De La Soul did sign with Rush, though not immediately after that show. It was after they had an album that was seeing some success. Throughout their career they've credited Simmons and Cohen for introducing them to the business side of making music, and for supporting sound decision-making along the way. Simmons "brought the business to everybody's talent," Maseo told *Juan Ep* in 2015.

July 3, 1988, the Jungle Brothers and De La Soul played a show together in Boston that was an important moment for both groups, and for hip-hop, kicking off the roots of the camaraderie that would become the Native Tongues collective.

Jungle Brothers were a New York group that embodied the Afrocentric direction within Black culture. They wore African fashions and had released their debut album *Straight out the Jungle* earlier that summer. Like De La Soul, they started as classmates. Founding members Mike G (Michael Small) and Afrika Baby Bam (Nathaniel Hall) went to high school together at Murry Bergtraum High School in Manhattan. Q-Tip and Ali Shaheed Muhammad (of A Tribe Called Quest) went to the same school, as did Jason Hunter (Brother J of X Clan). Brother J, Mike G, and Afrika Baby Bam would rap together. Brother J hosted talent shows at the high school, including the earliest performances of the group that became the Jungle Brothers.

Before Q-Tip had his own group, he was affiliated with Jungle Brothers. He appears on their songs "The Promo" and "Black Is Black." The latter he came up with and recorded on his own, as a demo, and then the group decided to redo it for their album. Afrika Baby Bam gave Q-Tip his rap name (before that he went by J Nice or MC Love Child) and suggested he add "A Tribe Called" to his planned group name Quest. Later, Afrika and Q-Tip would also come up with the collective name Native Tongues, to describe Jungle Brothers, Tribe, and De La.

Jungle Brothers were firmly within NYC hip-hop culture at the time, performing at the local clubs around town. DJ Red Alert was Mike G's uncle. De La Soul had seen the JBs perform at Latin Quarter and other New York nightclubs, and were big fans. They had a song they were working on for their second single that was patterned after a Jungle Brothers track. "Jenifa (Taught Me)" was envisioned as a sequel of sorts to the Jungle Brothers' "Jimbrowski."

The Boston show was an all-ages, afternoon appearance billed as Summer Jam Part II: The Out of School Boogie. On the bill were Finesse & Synquis, Jungle Brothers, Antoinette, and the local Boston group the Three Def Note$

(which included rapper Ed O.G., later of Ed O.G. & Da Bulldogs). The venue was the Channel (tagline: "Boston's best live rock"). The Jungle Brothers and De La Soul hung out together afterward and De La told them about "Jenifa." They exchanged phone numbers and hung out again the next day, at a show at Roy Wilkins Park in Queens where De La Soul performed "Potholes" and Jungle Brothers did some of their songs. That was also the first time De La met Q-Tip and Ali Shaheed Muhammad.

After those two shows, Q-Tip, De La, and the Jungle Brothers hung out often and invited each other to their studio sessions. As Phife of A Tribe Called Quest recounted to Brian Coleman in *Check the Technique*, "When Tip and the Jungle Brothers met up with De La it just seemed like they had known each other for years . . . it was just a family affair, not like a marketing thing." He compared it to elementary school sleepovers, but instead it would be in a recording studio. "We'd be in there all night, eating Chinese food and working."

De La Soul's second twelve-inch single, released August 1988, was a double A-side featuring "Jenifa (Taught Me)" and "Potholes in My Lawn." The B-side had instrumental versions of the two songs, given different titles ("Derwin" and "They Don't Know That the Soul Don't Go for That," respectively) and the one-minute bug-out "Skip 2 My Loop," a goof they made when a record started skipping.

"Jenifa" falls somewhere between an answer record—in dialogue with a previous record by another artist—and a tribute, to the Jungle Brothers' 1987 debut single "Jimbrowski," which had introduced the micro-trend of songs about "Jimmy" (penis) and "Jimmy hats" (condoms). See also Boogie Down Productions' "Jimmy," off their 1988 album

By All Means Necessary. DJ Red Alert told *Wax Poetics* that the term came from something his older brother would say.

"Jenifa" was the female version, but as Greg Tate describes in his essay "Yabba Dabba Doo-Wop: De La Soul," the song's attitude toward women and sex was atypical for the era. "De La Soul bow down to a horny female without passing judgment, showing a promiscuous biddy more respect than any brothers in hip-hop history." The song used as its base loop the 1965 single "Soupy" by Maggie Thrett, another 45 Pos found in his dad's collection.

Some of De La Soul's unique writing habits can be found on "Jenifa": the varied use of "De La" within other phrases ("lost in De La heaven"), the introduction of characters that sound fictional but are probably people they know (Derwin, the virgin in the song), creating their own slang and playing around with it ("just like Dan I strictly stuck"), taking an in-joke image and scattering it within songs ("I love daisies / read her shirt").

"Potholes in My Lawn" spawned the group's first video. They spent $800 on the mostly black-and-white clip, directed by Kevin Bray using an 8 mm camera. They rhyme in front of an Amityville house and dance with their friends, sometimes on an athletic field and sometimes near the water. It was the first high-profile video for Bray, who went on to direct music videos (for Whitney Houston, Celine Dion, Ben Folds Five, and more), TV shows, and movies. He told the website Shots.net that the De La video was "just digging in the dirt, using whatever we had in our hands."

"Jenifa" was added to the single because the group was concerned "Potholes" was too slow to be a hit. And "Potholes" does at first seem deeply weird, from the loping stroll to the yodeling background vocals. It exemplifies the group's enigmatic language, yet once you know the code, it's more straightforward than you think. It's a song about biters, telling other rappers not to mimic their style—in the lineage of Run-D.M.C.'s "Sucker M.C.'s." The lawn is their music, and the potholes are the holes left by other rappers stealing from them.

The first sound is the horns and then piano that start "Magic Mountain" by Eric Burdon and War. That song gives "Potholes" its essential groove, as well as one of its melodies. Another comes from "Synthetic Substitution," a 1973 song by Melvin Bliss that Ultramagnetic used in "Ego Trippin'" and which would become an ever more popular sample choice, especially the drums (see "O.P.P.," "DWYCK," "Bring Da Ruckus," and so on). The yodeling and twangy Jew's harp are from Parliament's "Little Ole Country Boy" off *Osmium*, their most Funkadelic-sounding album.

"Potholes" was another hit for the group, on radio and in clubs. It helped spread interest in De La Soul, as its video aired regionally on *Video Music Box* and nationally on *Yo! MTV Raps*. The success of the first two singles cemented the likelihood that De La Soul would get to make an album. Their Tommy Boy contract included the option for a second single, based on how the first did, and then the option for an album.

"Potholes in My Lawn" was later played on Mars in 2004, part of the playlist for NASA's Opportunity rover (which had its own LiveJournal, as OpportunityGrrl). Frequently described as the first hip-hop song played on Mars, "Potholes" was actually the first hip-hop song not by the Beastie Boys played on Mars. "Body Movin'" was played forty-seven days earlier (forty-seven Mars days, each forty minutes longer than an Earth day).

4. EYES WIDE OPEN: *3 FEET HIGH AND RISING* AND THE D.A.I.S.Y. AGE

Even before De La Soul released their second single, Tommy Boy sent them on the road. "Plug Tunin'" was being played in Texas, so the label booked a gig in Houston. It was their first appearance outside the East Coast. August 18, 1988, they played on a bill with Sir Mix-a-Lot and the Geto Boys at the Rhinestone Wrangler, the first all-rap venue in Houston and the center of the local scene. There was a relationship between NYC and the Houston scene at the time, largely due to James Prince, the Houston entrepreneur who was inspired by Def Jam and formed the Rap-A-Lot label in 1986. He had explored starting the label in New York before bringing it back to Houston. The members of De La Soul hadn't traveled much and were a bit shocked to see the scene in Houston. "You would have thought we went to Mars," Trugoy told the *Juan Ep* podcast in 2015. University of Houston Library's Houston Hip Hop Research Collection has a copy of the "contract" for the show—a letter from Tommy Boy's Dante Ross to the promoter, Steve Fournier, confirming that the group agreed to perform for free, if all travel and expenses were provided for.

In the last few months of 1988 and into 1989, De La

Soul were taking any concert opportunity that came their way. They performed various shows with the Jungle Brothers on the East Coast and played their first West Coast show in Los Angeles at the roller rink World on Wheels. While there they met a pre–Cypress Hill B-Real and got exposed to the Crips and Bloods of L.A. when an audience tussle interrupted their performance. They did shows with Too Short and Three Times Dope, Young MC, and Kid 'n Play. They joined the 2 Live Crew's Move Somethin' tour, with Tone Loc, EPMD, Tuff Crew, MC Shy D, and Rob Base & DJ E-Z Rock.

The D.A.I.S.Y. Age arrived in early 1989, with De La Soul's Day-Glo-colored debut album *3 Feet High and Rising*. It would break their career, cement their legacy, and be recognized twenty-one years later by the Library of Congress as part of the National Recording Registry, intended to preserve recordings that are "culturally, historically, or aesthetically significant."

When the group started, making an album wasn't really in their consciousness. "Success for us was hearing Mr. Magic say, 'World-world premiere,'" Posdnuos told the *Drink Champs* podcast in 2019. All three members of De La Soul had concrete plans for their adult lives; none saw their future as being professional musicians. Trugoy was at architectural school. Posdnuos was headed to college, to study music business and audio engineering. Mase was still finishing up high school, and planning to enter the army afterward. They all put their life plans on hold when Tommy Boy asked them to make an album.

The years 1987–1988 saw the release of what now seems like a dizzying array of classic albums. From spring 1988 to the end of the year brought EPMD's *Strictly Business*,

Stetsasonic's *In Full Gear*, Big Daddy Kane's *Long Live the Kane*, Public Enemy's *It Takes a Nation of Millions to Hold Us Back*, Eric B. & Rakim's *Follow the Leader*, Salt-N-Pepa's *A Salt with a Deadly Pepa*, Eazy-E's *Eazy-Duz-It*, MC Lyte's *Lyte as a Rock*, Kid 'n Play's *2 Hype*, Ultramagnetic MCs' *Critical Beatdown*, Slick Rick's *The Great Adventures of Slick Rick*, Jungle Brothers' *Straight out the Jungle*, and much more. Call it a golden era or simply a genre growing up, it felt like a new earthquaking debut or second album was being released every week.

It was a time when rap album success was becoming a thing, and artists were figuring out how to express themselves in the format. Run-D.M.C. had smash albums earlier, but artists across '87 and '88 were learning how to construct an album start to finish, more conceptually as one piece. *It Takes a Nation* was the great leap forward in that regard. In its sampling approach and overall construction, it's a clear precursor to what De La Soul were about to do.

3 Feet High and Rising was completed in just over one month's time, at Calliope Studios, where they had worked on the demo and singles. They were finished recording by the end of August 1988, and it was released in February '89 (despite being often listed as March 3; rap release history is slippery). Originally the album was supposed to be out in September, two weeks after the "Jenifa"/"Potholes" single, but the label decided to wait until there were fewer competing new releases. A "genius move," Dante Ross told Brian Coleman in *Check the Technique*.

The overall budget for the album was somewhere between $13,000 and $20,000. They often recorded overnight, to save money, and used cheaper reels of tape for recording. The studio recording experience was the outgrowth of their creative explorations. Prince Paul and De La Soul came to the studio with a notebook of ideas and dozens of songs that were largely completed, in four-track form. They'd record them primitively at Prince Paul's home studio—nicknamed "Paul's Coffee Shop" after an empty shop they'd walk past near their school.

In that way they did as much "preproduction" as possible, bringing the basic songs and then experimenting with them in the studio. Part of the process was getting used to more professional equipment. As they tried out the greater array of tools and equipment, they asked a lot of questions. "When you constantly ask questions, you start to find out answers," Prince Paul told Red Bull Music Academy in 2003.

As with the demo and singles, they had twenty-four tracks to work with instead of just four. Prince Paul told Mase to think of the channels on the board as separate car stereos playing different pieces of the song at the same time. They got used to recording vocals in a vocal booth. Before working in a studio, they would stand in the corner of a room and rhyme into one microphone.

In the *Frank151* article about Calliope, Sue Wright describes how simple the studio's technology for recording samples was at the time De La Soul recorded there: "one little drum machine and a sync tone . . . to tell the drum machine when to start . . . and one little sampling machine," an Akai S900.

There was also a pitch shifter, an Eventide Harmonizer, which they started using. Both Prince Paul and Posdnuos have described this as an important moment in the evolution of De La Soul. They figured out that if one sample, whether of a vocal or music, wasn't in the same key as the others, they could use the Harmonizer to shift the key, to get all the samples to gel. Everything was a mystery they were trying to solve. "You had to invent this," Prince Paul told RBMA in 2003.

Trugoy told *Juan Ep* they came in with so many notes and ideas that "it was actually easy, doing an album." The songs came quickly. They recorded the album version of "The Magic Number" in one day. In a 2013 interview for the *Soundtrack Series* podcast, Posdnuos described Calliope as having a vibe that felt like home. "So that played a part in how we comfortably made music and came up with ideas while there," he remembered. "There were no rules because we didn't know them."

Under Prince Paul's guidance, they would also try things out on the fly. On "Jenifa Taught Me," what sounds like tambourines being played are handfuls of coins, shaken near a microphone. If someone had an idea, they would test it to see if it would work. Any idea was worth exploring. They didn't have an overall concept for the album in mind yet. They took each idea at a time, each song at a time. If they made a mistake while recording, they would leave it in if it sounded cool enough. In a March 1989 cover story for *The Source*, Trugoy described their evolution in making music together: "The more we grew, the more we worked together, the better our sound became."

Prince Paul was thought of as the producer, and credited that way on the album, but the musical ideas came from all four of them. As with all De La Soul's early songwriting, the songs grew from specific musical or conceptual ideas that the individual members brought as a starting place. "Do As De La Does," "Tread Water," and "Can U Keep a Secret" started out as tracks Prince Paul had put together for Stetsasonic's *In Full Gear* album which that group rejected.

"Eye Know" came from Pos wanting to sample Steely Dan's "Peg," ever since hearing it on AM radio, at home and over the mall loudspeakers while he worked at Burger King. He made a loop of it while Prince Paul had a couple of days away playing shows with Stetsasonic, and they finished the track when he returned. A brief whistle from Otis Redding's "Sitting on the Dock of the Bay" is used in the song to emulate a flute.

For "The Magic Number," back at Mase's house when they were first playing around with records, they had joined together "Multiplication Rock" from TV's *Schoolhouse Rock* with a breakbeat that Double Dee & Steinski used on 1985's "Lesson 3 (History of Hip Hop Mix)" (itself built from Led Zeppelin's "The Crunge"). The song's Johnny Cash sample, which gave the album its name, was brought by Trugoy, who found it in his father's record collection. The vast majority of the records they used on *3 Feet High and Rising* came from their parents' collections, with some additions from Prince Paul.

The final minute of "Magic Number" demonstrates the glee in which they would combine unlikely sources—scratching from the Skinny Boys asking, "Yo, what's up?" to Jam Master Jay's "1-2-3" to NYC mayor Fiorello La Guardia's "I say children, what does it all mean?" to Rudy Ray Moore's "I wouldn't lie to you" to Fatback asking "Is this the future?" to Syl Johnson's "Different Strokes" ("do the shing-a-ling") to Eddie Murphy asking, "Anybody in the audience ever get hit by a car?" to Johnny Cash singing about how high the water is, and back to *Schoolhouse Rock*. The La Guardia sample smuggled its way in as a part of the Double Dee & Steinski sample, along with a clip from the movie *Putney Swope*.

"Cool Breeze on the Rocks" went further in the number of back-to-back samples, with a quick flurry of around twenty. Richard Pryor saying "cool breezes" leads to a whole succession of songs mentioning "rock" in some fashion. Tracks by Public Enemy, Vaughan Mason & Crew, MC Lyte, Cerrone, the Fearless Four, the Rock Steady Crew, Afrika Bambaataa & Soulsonic Force, Crash Crew, Cutmaster D.C., Steady B, Run-D.M.C, Jefferson Starship, Gregory Abbott, Beastie Boys, Orange Krush, the Treacherous Three, the Real Roxanne, the B Boys, Michael Jackson, and LL Cool J. It's a sound collage that strings together its own melody while experimenting with juxtaposition, in under one minute.

In the introduction to his book *Bring That Beat Back: How Sampling Built Hip-Hop*, Nate Patrin describes "the power of recontextualization" that sampling has; the ability to take disparate pieces of music and put them together as something new. He writes, "Hip-hop reframed music as the meritocracy that charts, labels, and the industry couldn't." *3 Feet High and Rising* exemplifies those concepts. The group sampled anything they could find, from any era, that they thought worked in their songs.

Their approach to layering samples was unique at the time. Public Enemy's was closest in terms of combining multiple, seemingly unconnected sources of music and layering them over each other. The standard approach in the late eighties was to choose a breakbeat and maybe another sample as a hook, with James Brown a staple. In 1991 Pos described their approach to sampling this way to *Keyboard* magazine: "A lot of the hip-hop records that are out consist of about three loops as far as the music goes—the melody, the beat, and maybe something else. We usually have about seven loops, all these little melodies, always adding things on top of that hard beat."

A good example is "Say No Go." Its title phrase is the obvious sample. In 1982, "I Can't Go for That (No Can Do)" by Daryl Hall & John Oates was the only song that hit #1 on both the pop and R&B charts that year. De La Soul uses it as an antidrug message, grabbing on to the three words Hall sings at the end of each verse (as in, "Don't even think about it / say no go"). Beyond that sample, there are drums from the Rolling Stones' "Honky Tonk Women," a bit from Sly Stone's "Crossword Puzzle" that they use as a recurring lead-in to the chorus, and the hooky guitar that kicked off Detroit Emeralds' "Baby Let Me Take You (In My Arms)."

It's an antidrug song with visceral imagery (a baby born to drug addicts "would have asked the nurse for a hit" if they could talk at birth). But it's also about trying to comprehend it all; in his verse Posdnuos keeps rewinding and rephrasing to find the right words, but he can't get there: "push couldn't shove me to understand."

Trugoy told *Rolling Stone* the song came from the sample first. The phrase "say no go" caught their attention, so they built a song around what that phrase might mean. It became a "message" song of sorts, but it started with a few words drawn from a song of the past.

"Ghetto Thang" is another track in a serious vein that started with the music, originally an idea from Trugoy. In a song-by-song breakdown of the album in *Rolling Stone*, Posdnuos shared that "Ghetto Thang" was originally titled "Soft Violins," after the name of a preprogrammed keyboard sound Trugoy was messing with at Mase's house. Over time they gave it a better beat, changed up the sound, and added more serious lyrics to show another side of the group. Less than a mile from their area of Amityville was a block filled with crack dealers. Even in the suburbs they observed and experienced the urban social ills of the moment: drug addiction, homelessness, the way drugs and the criminal justice system tore Black families apart.

Songs with a social message weren't the norm on *3 Feet High and Rising*, which overall resembled a cross among a party, a children's fable, a creative writing competition, and a comedy sketch show. Even before meeting Prince Paul, the group had messed around with skits when they were making music at home. "Bug-out pieces," they called them. Adding them to *3 Feet High and Rising* was Prince Paul's idea, to keep the flow of the album moving and add an entertainment factor. Without the skits, it felt more serious, slower, more densely packed. The skits amplified the humor and playfulness of the songs and allowed more breathing room between their rhymes.

The skits largely take the format of a game show, with one of the mixing engineers, Al Watts, serving as the game show host. "He was a white guy with the perfect voice," Prince Paul told *Complex* in 2011. Paul's friend and frequent collaborator Don Newkirk is the announcer. The idea behind the game show was to introduce the members of De La Soul in a humorous way, to give a sense of their personalities. As a listener, if you felt like you knew them, almost like they were your own goofy friends, you'd be more open to the inside jokes and the odd twists and turns.

Though De La Soul and Prince Paul introduced and popularized the use of skits on hip-hop albums, they can't take credit for having the very first hip-hop skit to be released, per Jeff Weiss's "A History of the Hip Hop Skit," a

2015 article for RBMA. While they were working on *3 Feet High*, King Tee was on the West Coast recording "Baggin' on Moms," which made it to the marketplace a few months earlier, on his album *Act a Fool*.

The game show within the album consists of four ridiculous questions: How many feathers are on a Perdue chicken? How many fibers are intertwined in a shredded wheat biscuit? What does *tush eht lleh pu* mean? How many times did the Batmobile catch a flat? None of the contestants get it right so, at the end of the album, listeners are told to write their answers on a postcard and send them to the Tommy Boy office (1747 First Avenue) c/o Dante the Scrubb.

Pos told Angus Batey for HipHop.com, "It was a real competition, but no one really got it right!" It led to a stack of mail on Dante Ross's desk that he may or may not have ever looked through. The questions and answers, really the whole game show, was a Prince Paul idea with improvised input from the others. Even De La Soul aren't sure of the answers to the questions. Pos said, "The fibers in a shredded wheat biscuit? I have no fucking idea! I think that was just Paul being an idiot."

Dante the Scrubb was Dante Ross. It was an affectionate joke, which is how De La Soul has characterized it. Dante Ross has said it's something *he'd* call *them*, so they were getting him back. However, he's given different stories about the circumstances (he'd call them "scrubs" during basketball games; he called them "scrubs" because they wouldn't get into a swimming pool, etc.). Prince Paul has painted it differently, saying that it was because Ross represented the label, the establishment, the man, and the group felt like he was there to spy on them and make sure they were doing what they should. The way the comic strip in the album's liner notes depicts Dante the Scrubb backs up Prince Paul's take. Dante, a duck, is worried that they won't get the album done in time: "If not, my superior Monica will have my head."

For the record, *tush eht lleh pu* is "shut the hell up" backward, more or less. Comic book enthusiasts online say the Batmobile caught a flat at least twice in the comics, but there are so many Batman versions that it's hard to say definitively. In *Frank151*, they give supposed answers to the questions, albeit in foreign languages that translate into non-answers. How many fibers? "I can't tell you." Feathers on a Perdue chicken? "Sorry, I'm a vegetarian."

Prince Paul advocated for giving every track, even a short skit, a name—to make the album feel more abundant to music buyers. Along with the skits themselves were songs that were like semi-skits. These short tunes had elements of a song, but still were mostly "bug outs." "A Little Bit of Soap," a quick body-odor joke, was something Pos came up with after hearing "A Little Bit of Soap" by the Jarmels—likely another record from his dad's collection—and wanting to do something with it. "I Can Do Anything (Delacratic)" goofs around with their theme of individual freedom, backed with beatboxing by Wise from Stetsasonic. "Description," a minute and a half of introductions from the album's cast of characters, was produced by Q-Tip, who also wrote the song's rhymes.

Another of the semi-skits, "De La Orgee," came simply from Prince Paul having a Barry White beat he thought sounded like porno music. Everyone in the studio that day gathered around one mic to imitate the sounds of an orgy. "I was surprised how much they got into it!" Paul told Open

Mike Eagle on the *What Had Happened Was* podcast.

The scene in the recording studio often resembled a party. De La Soul would invite their friends to come by and hang out during the recording sessions. And if they were there, they'd find a way onto a song. Pos put it this way in a 2021 *Chicago Reader* conversation with the artist Rhymefest: "Whoever's in the studio—yo, if you in the studio, man, you are gonna wind up on the record." For example, the crowd on "Do as De La Does" includes DJ Red Alert, Chris Ali of the Violators, MC Lyte, and Q-Tip.

That's how "Buddy," the "posse cut" that stands as the birth of the Native Tongues, came to be: the right people in the right place on the right day. It featured guest verses from Q-Tip and the Jungle Brothers, but it wasn't planned that way. That song wasn't intended to have guests on it at all. It came from friends hanging out in the studio. The day De La Soul recorded "Buddy" happened to be the day they invited the Jungle Brothers and Q-Tip to hang out in the studio, not long after the July shows in Boston and Queens. If they had come by the day before, they might have ended up on "Ghetto Thang."

Mase liked to play "Girl, I Think the World about You" by the Commodores over and over in the studio. He was playing it one day and Trugoy impulsively started singing "meanie meanie" over it in the same way he ended up doing on "Buddy." The lyrics take the "Jenifa" and "Jimmy" concepts and create a related slang word. In De La speak, "buddy" means "body," but it also suggests the merging of bodies, so to speak.

On the album they redid the main songs from the twelve-inch singles, adding new elements or treating them like either sequels or rewrites. "Plug Tunin'" was now "Plug

Tunin' (Last Chance to Comprehend)." Prince Paul added a new vocal sample to open the song. It's something he found at Island Media, the studio where they were mixing the album. It's Liberace, from *The Liberace Show*, declaring, "And now, for my next number I'd like to return to the classics, perhaps the most famous classic in all the world of music." For Liberace, that's a setup to then play "Chopsticks," to audience laughter. For De La Soul it's also a joke, and a playful boast, reintroducing their introductory single as if it's already world-famous.

The album's version of "Plug Tunin'" resembles a sequel. So does "Jenifa Taught Me (Derwin's Revenge)," with a new section where Derwin, the virgin, gets revenge by showing off his skill, "something Jenny could never do": playing "Chopsticks" on the piano. The way the piano interlude disrupts the song is indicative of the mood of the album. From the skits to the cartoonish stories in songs like "Tread Water," characters are continually coming and going.

"Freedom of Speak" became "Change in Speak," a completely different song but with similarities in the rhyme style—the repetition of the same rhyming sound at the end of each line in a verse.

The three members of De La Soul were eighteen years old, two of them soon turning nineteen, when recording *3 Feet High*. Juvenile humor was at play, with songs about body odor and sex merging with their habit of creating their own language and in-jokes. Even songs that came across to the listener as making a serious point were created as jokes that doubled as rap sketchbooks, places to play around with different ways to rhyme, and unlikely combinations of sounds.

For example, "Take It Off" came from Pos's younger

brother being in the studio and jokingly saying "take it off" in a style similar to the song "Kick the Ball" by the Krown Rulers, a Philadelphia-area hit at the time. So they decided to try it out as a song. They list off fashion trends they are tired of, in an on-the-fly way that comes off like a serious proclamation, though they're clearly trying to be funny.

The animal fable "Tread Water" could be seen as silly or serious, and over the years the group has vacillated on which they think it is. Pos used to say it was the song he hated most, but in recent years has mentioned it as one of his favorites, citing its positive message of perseverance. In the track they take on different animal personas, almost like they're reenacting a *Zoobilee Zoo* episode.

An idea the group had played around with from an earlier time was that of the D.A.I.S.Y. Age. Part and parcel with the meaning behind the group's name, it was intended to reflect them following their inner creative spirit. D.A.I.S.Y. was an acronym for Da Inner Sound Y'all. (DJ Stitches told *Unkut* it originally stood for Da Ill Shit Y'all.)

The D.A.I.S.Y. Age idea came from Trugoy wondering how to incorporate a cool image after seeing a Mickey Mouse shirt with a daisy on it at Macy's. "What could a daisy mean and be really cool?" he wondered, per a 2016 *Uncut* article. "We were just kids who saw things a different way. We were obviously eyes wide open." On the comedy podcast *The Champs*, in 2014, Mase articulated the "inner sound" concept like this: "a sound from within us that's just true and honest, letting out every emotion of who we are as people."

The daisies were a visual idea that Tommy Boy grabbed onto for the artwork and the promotion of the album, which used sixties connotations and suggested De La Soul were flower children. Tommy Boy placed ads oriented toward a rock 'n' roll audience. One magazine ad showed a young white man in a suit and tie, apparently on his way out of a record store, with the tagline, "I came in for U2, I came out with De La Soul." Underneath was a quote from the *Los Angeles Times* calling the album "The *Sergeant Pepper's* of the eighties." Another apparent target audience was Black women who liked R&B, or the radio stations they listened to. A similar ad in *Billboard* had a woman holding the record, with another tagline: "I came in for Patti LaBelle, I came out with De La Soul." (The woman was Rita Owens, Queen Latifah's mom.)

Toby Mott, part of the London-based design firm the Grey Organisation, created the album cover. He had worked with Tommy Boy before, art-directing the music video for the Information Society's "What's on Your Mind (Pure Energy)." For the *3 Feet* cover, the firm was paid a one-off fee of roughly $2,000, per an interview in *The Guardian*. It was a black-and-white photo of the trio, taken from a ladder while they were laying on the floor. Mott put the bright-colored drawings of flowers and lettering over it—using liquid paint and Posca paint pens to draw on the acetate of the photo. Mott wrote in an essay about the experience that he didn't have the hippie angle in mind. Instead, the intent was "to be new and bright, with the overlaying of the fluorescent flowers and text reflecting a synthetic pop cartoon look." The album art is in the collection of the Museum of Modern Art, the only hip-hop album artwork in their collection.

The last song De La Soul recorded for the album was "This Is a Recording 4 Living in a Fulltime Era (L.I.F.E.)." Pos has said he heard an early version of *The Great Adventures of Slick Rick* while they were finalizing the album, and he was so in awe of it he started to question the quality of their own LP. He came up with one more song that was tougher-sounding, to round out the record. The rhymes, back and forth between Pos and Trugoy, maintain their full-time commitment to rap as a way of life and a mission. The track combines elements of "Mt. Airy Groove" by Pieces of a Dream with the breakbeat from "Action" by Orange Krush. The "this is a recording" spoken vocal is from "Got to Get a Knutt" by New Birth.

The album was almost finished when the record label asked them to create a song that sounded more like a single. The second-to-last song they recorded for the album would become their biggest hit: "Me Myself and I." The song was rooted in Mase and Prince Paul's mutual love for George Clinton.

One of Prince Paul's main musical obsessions as a kid was Parliament-Funkadelic. He would skip school to listen to P-Funk in his bedroom. He nearly flunked sixth grade because he spent too much time listening to the Parliament album *Motor Booty Affair*. P-Funk was also one of Mase's earliest obsessions. In 1976, when he was six years old, his mom and uncle took him to see P-Funk land their Mothership in Central Park ("one of the best nights of my life, as a kid," he told *Serato Unscripted*).

3 Feet has a clear P-Funk thread running through it. The character names, the artwork, the strangeness. Prince Paul told Angus Batey at HipHip.com, "This gave me an opportunity to make my Parliament-Funkadelic record, and that's what *3 Feet High and Rising* was."

Mase had for a long time wanted to build a song off a sample of "(Not Just) Knee Deep" by Funkadelic, a fifteen-minute jam on their 1979 album *Uncle Jam Wants You*. It's a song that George Clinton himself described in his memoir as an attempt "to identify and isolate the essence of P-Funk." It was one of the first songs Mase had messed around with when he was learning to DJ. He and Prince Paul worked together on getting the track right.

The emcees took more convincing. They came up with an idea for the rhymes quickly, just to get something done, still thinking (or hoping) the song might not end up on the album. Their idea was to build the rhyming cadence, Trugoy's especially, off the Jungle Brothers' "Black Is Black"—something nodded to overtly with Q-Tip's appearance on the song ("I point to Tip and he says, 'Black is black'").

The "Me Myself and I" video is a school detention scenario where the teacher and students are practicing the rap clichés of the day. Prince Paul, in a suit and tie, does a *Twilight Zone*–ish intro where he tells a riddle or something: "If you take three glasses of water and put food coloring in them, you have many different colors, but it's still the same old water."

Trugoy and Pos have pointed out in interviews how different the video portrayal was from their actual school life. In the video they're outsiders, from their haircuts to their clothes to their demeanor. However, they were popular kids, active in school. The school in the video represents conformity in hip-hop trends. The teacher, Professor DefBeat, is showing the kids how to wear their gold chains and Kangol hats, and how to stand. De La fail each test.

"Proud I'm proud is what I am," Trugoy rhymes, standing like he's reading an essay the teacher assigned him to write. The concept and video are perfectly matched to the sentiment of the song: "Style is surely our own thing / not the false disguise of showbiz."

It was released as a single on February 14, 1989, and was a hit by all measures: sales, chart, radio, and critics. And it drove the success of the album, which started moving up the charts along with it. "Me Myself and I" was a song and video combination that perfectly crystallized an already emerging impression of the group's personality. From the early singles, De La Soul already presented as a different sort of group, creating their own universe in song. "Me Myself and I" told listeners not just that they were going to be themselves, in opposition of societal and industry trends, but that everyone else should be themselves too.

A jokey B-side, "Brain Washed Follower," featured a kid named Jeff (voiced by Trugoy's cousin) making fun of De La Soul for not doing the things he thinks rappers should do: carrying beepers, wearing gold chains, driving expensive cars. Jeff appeared again on the B-side "The Mack Daddy on the Left" (from the "Say No Go" twelve-inch) rapping about curfews, hand-holding, and respecting your parents ("they're pushovers") over cool piano from Dr. Buzzard's Original Savannah Band.

There's a three-groove version of the twelve-inch single that Tommy Boy made as a gimmick, or a dare to do something different. The B-side has two separate grooves cut into it; where the needle is placed determines which song is heard.

The group told *Drink Champs* Tommy Boy projected fifty thousand units of *3 Feet High and Rising* would be sold. It sold over one hundred thousand copies in two weeks' time, hitting gold status (five hundred thousand sold) on May 30, 1989. The single "Me Myself and I" was certified gold one month later. *3 Feet* officially achieved platinum status in 2000, though the group believes it hit that status earlier.

The success of the song, album, and group had an almost immediate impact on the lives and futures of many subsets of listeners, including aspiring artists who saw that they could do their own thing. Questlove of the Roots told the *New York Times* podcast *Popcast* in 2023 that "literally all bullying in [his] life stopped" when "Me Myself and I" came out. His former bullies recognized in him what they saw in De La Soul: "Oh, you nerds are cool." In the book *Check the Technique*, Ishmael "Butterfly" Butler of Digable Planets and Shabazz Palaces said hearing *3 Feet High and Rising* "sparked something" in him, realizing he could make rap music with the originality he associated with the avant-garde jazz his dad listened to. Mike D of the Beastie Boys told interviewer Angus Batey he was "crushed" when he heard *3 Feet* because it was so similar to what they were trying to do on their not-yet-released album *Paul's Boutique* and beat them to the punch. Within a few years' span, there would be a bounty of groups and albums from which you could draw a connection, intentional or not, back to De La's approach: Arrested Development, P.M. Dawn, Freestyle Fellowship, the Pharcyde, the Roots, and more.

The 1989 Pazz & Jop poll, the annual poll of music critics run by the *Village Voice*, ranked *3 Feet High and Rising* as album of the year. It was the first winner not distributed by a major label since the poll began in 1971. While Robert Christgau's accompanying essay called hip-hop "the new punk"—insinuating it captivated critics looking for something original to vote for—he also downplayed the extent to which De La Soul was a part of the larger hip-hop community. "These three suburban teenagers rapped without swagger or inferable threat," he wrote, "their dumb humor and original sound were out there for all to hear." Christgau was surprised *3 Feet High and Rising* came out on top; he felt it "was just too slight to go all the way."

Critics loved the album, but the vast majority used the sixties as a reference point. De La Soul were "hippie-hop," making "the first psychedelic hip-hop record," wrote Michael Azerrad in *Rolling Stone*. They reminded critics of humorists: Monty Python, the Firesign Theatre, Cheech & Chong. Critics showed their hand a bit by not mentioning any Black comedians, not even those whose voices appeared on the album itself: Richard Pryor, Eddie Murphy, Rudy Ray Moore.

Richard Cromelin of the *Los Angeles Times* called the LP "something closer to sixties Mothers of Invention than eighties Run-D.M.C.," a misreading of both De La Soul's relationship to hip-hop and of the genre itself. In a May 1989 *Washington Post* article, Richard Harrington hit all the touchpoints, calling the album "the dizziest hour this side of Monty Python" and an album that if released in 1969 "might have been called *Sgt. Salt 'n' Pepa*."

The British music press took the hippie angle even further, setting up De La Soul in opposition with other rap music along the way. In *Melody Maker*, David Stubbs gave the backhanded compliment, "If Hip Hop has a future, it's De La Soul." Also for *Melody Maker*, writing about De La Soul, Push (the pseudonym of Christopher Dawes) wrote, "Rap is still commonly perceived as a cliched musical genre involving little beyond dissing and bragging, vandalism and sexism, negativity with a JB beat jolt."

De La Soul grew frustrated with the incessant comparisons to the hippie movement and having a florist at every photo shoot, ready to dress them in flowers. They knew Tommy Boy viewed the hippie angle as a path to broader popularity. In a 2016 *Breakfast Club* interview, Trugoy said, "Let's just say it, it was something for the white audience to associate with."

In July 1989, De La Soul played the *Arsenio Hall Show*. Arsenio introduced them like this: "I like to call them the hippies of hip-hop. Their brand of psychedelic rap has helped this album, *3 Feet High and Rising*, climb to the top of the charts." During their performance, Maseo dropped the music out to highlight the song's lyric, "You say Plug 1 and 2 are hippies; no, we're not, that's pure plug bull." Their frustration with people calling them hippies was already built into the song. On *Arsenio* they also incorporated the music and lyrics from the B-side, "Ain't Hip to Be Labeled a Hippie," where they declare, "Daisies don't mean everything / daisies don't mean anything." In the "Me Myself and I" video, Pos pushes away the embodiment of the hippie, comedian Jim Turner's Randee of the Redwoods character, who was a constant presence on MTV as a cartoonish representation of the past.

Trugoy told the *NME*, about the incessant use of the word "hippie" by the music media: "I feel like we're trapped in that word, can't escape. . . . You can't trap us in one word because we're hundreds and thousands of words." Soon enough the group would turn that feeling of entrapment against the hit single they felt obligated to perform, incorporating a "we hate this song" chant that has remained in their performances of it throughout their career.

Critics struggled to find a frame of reference for De La Soul that didn't involve flowers and peace references, and translating that to "hippie." A *Boston Globe* concert review by Jim Sullivan captured the dilemma writers were in. The group disavowed from stage the idea that they were hippies, but "it does make you wonder why they wear flowery print shirts and sling the phrase 'This is the daisy age' on their records." The same review expressed agreement with a relayed John Lydon quote that De La was closer to *Sesame Street* than Public Enemy—meant to be a compliment, apparently. (Lydon also said most rap was "just some big mouth yelling at you.")

De La Soul was intent on demonstrating that their music was using the past to get to the future. Pos told *Rolling Stone*, "We are going back to the sixties, but also to the seventies, the fifties, the eighties, and on to the future."

The "hippie" idea followed the trio everywhere they went, and was perhaps a factor in a piece of trivia that runs counter to the public perception of their music: they were kicked off their first national tour because they kept getting into fistfights.

After the release and success of the album, they spent over a year on tour, across the second half of 1989 and much of 1990. First was LL Cool J's Nitro tour, presented by Rush Artist Management. LL Cool J was the headliner, with the other main acts including Big Daddy Kane, Slick Rick, N.W.A., Too Short, and De La Soul—with EPMD, Special Ed, and others appearing on some dates. De La performed first, often when the lights were still on and people were just starting to trickle in. Yet being included in the tour was a big deal to the members of De La Soul. They were touring with artists they looked up to, and they were learning from them about the business and about performing live.

The 1989 N.W.A. tour scenes depicted in the 2015 biopic *Straight Outta Compton* were during the Nitro tour.

The hotel shenanigans in Houston, the Cincinnati moment where they got a letter from the FBI, the Philadelphia Spectrum show, the Detroit set cut short during their performance of "Fuck tha Police"—De La Soul was around for all those events. Imagine them as invisible characters in the movie, and it might mess with your preconceived notions about East Coast / West Coast rap and about "positive" rap music versus "gangsta rap." As Mase told *The Barbershop Show* podcast in 2015, "That East-West thing was a fallacy; it didn't really exist" at that point in time. N.W.A. and De La Soul were friends on the tour. They'd hang out, party together, kill time together. "We clicked the most," Posdnuos told Headkrack on a *Dish Nation* interview in 2015. "Eazy-E and Cube, we would go to the mall together."

They left the Nitro tour early, at the request of the organizers, because they kept getting into fights along the way. "We was the fighters, all day," Trugoy told the *Juan Ep* podcast. Some of it was people in certain cities testing the group because their image made them expect De La Soul to be soft. But it was also the sense of loyalty that De La had, having the backs of the other artists if someone wanted to fight them. Some fights were an outgrowth of the parties and shenanigans after the shows. Every night during "Smooth Operator," Big Daddy Kane would give the name of the hotel the groups were staying at and invite women to come by.

The tour after that was supporting the Fine Young Cannibals. On the Nitro tour they were playing to largely Black audiences in US cities, and felt appreciated, even if they also felt like their live set wasn't quite up to snuff. On the Fine Young Cannibals tour, "hardly anyone knew who the hell we were," Mase told *NME*. It was an older, whiter crowd. Trugoy nearly quit the tour partway through because he was having trouble dealing with playing for audiences that didn't know their music. Russell Simmons called and talked him into staying the course.

They then toured England, Europe, and Japan—all essentially in a row. Mase was the youngest of the group, and hadn't yet finished high school. Russell Simmons and Lyor Cohen went to Mase's parents, and to the Board of Education, to get approval for him to go on the overseas tour. They made an agreement that he'd do his homework from the road, get everything turned in on time, so he could still graduate. After each show he would go back to the hotel to do schoolwork.

Their stage show wasn't yet what it would become. They struggled to create a live show that fit the expectations given by their album. They were imitating the artists they loved watching—KRS-One, Stetsasonic—while their music was begging for a different approach. These tours were where they learned how to build an effective setlist, how to get the crowd interested and keep them engaged. This would set the group up for decades of touring the US and the world. They became known for their audience-participation-heavy live sets. De La Soul would ultimately follow the example of their peers Public Enemy, Ice T, and Cypress Hill by playing shows across the globe, on varied lineups, and all of that started back in 1989, when their live show "sucked" (their own description).

Mase has talked about this period of the group's career as quick-moving, and as a turning point that determined the entire trajectory of his life. He told *Vibe*: "We were fresh out of high school and fresh off the block, making that transition if we were going to be hustlers or were we going to be in this rap thing? I was dealing with some issues in my life where I was involved with the streets heavy. I was a big part of the welfare system. Now, here comes this turning point in my life with this hip-hop shit."

5. SHADES OF BLACK COMPLEXITY: THE NATIVE TONGUES COLLECTIVE

An iconic line in "Buddy" was delivered by Afrika Baby Bam of the Jungle Brothers: "De La Soul / from the soul / black medallions / no gold."

Among Black youth it was a trend of the moment, above and beyond hip-hop. In April 1989, the *Washington Post* article "A Proud Fashion Statement" described African medallions as "a major fashion trend, perhaps with political undertones," declaring that the medallions "seem to have appeared overnight on Black teenagers." Some of the medallion wearers in the article connected it to Afrocentric education, to learning more about their heritage and history. Others mentioned seeing the medallions on hip-hop artists, but not yet De La Soul. The examples cited are Public Enemy, Salt 'N' Pepa, Just-Ice, and the Jungle Brothers, along with nonmusic celebrities Arsenio Hall and Robert Townsend.

Part of the concept of the "Me Myself and I" video was to play up the contrast between De La Soul and the look of the day. While the three members of the group were wearing multiple leather necklaces, with medallions showing Africa, all their classmates had on ridiculously sized gold chains (peep the memorable coon-skin cap and gold chain look of actor Sylvester Covin).

The media coverage of De La Soul's early success focused on their Afrocentric look as an intentional contrast to that of other hip-hop artists, to the point that the group became frustrated. Mase told the *NME*'s Sean O'Hagan the black medallions weren't something they invented but were part of the culture: "Bambaataa been wearin' them for years. The Zulu Nation been carrying those symbols for years before us. Our ancestors been wearing them from time."

The Afrocentricity, and related style, of what came to be called the Native Tongues can be connected back to Afrika Bambaataa and the Zulu Nation, something Mase and Afrika Baby Bam have mentioned in interviews. Bambaataa, a member of the Black Spades street gang, started the Zulu Nation in 1973, to steer warring Black and Puerto Rican gangs in the Bronx toward creative outlets and community building. The most musically eclectic of hip-hop's "founding fathers," he set the template for omnivorous listening translated into creative output. Prince Paul has described Bambaataa's record collection as the best of any DJ, one that made him want to seek out unusual music. He introduced hip-hop culture to the punk and art scenes of downtown Manhattan, and he built the Zulu Nation into a hip-hop movement. As Jeff Chang phrased it in *Can't Stop Won't Stop: A History of the Hip-Hop Generation*, "Bambaataa took Herc's party and turned it into the ceremony of a new faith, like he knew that this was exactly how their world was supposed to look, sound and flow."

There's a record from 1972, New Birth's "African Cry," that came to mind for Q-Tip one night in 1988, when he and Afrika Baby Bam were thinking of a collective name to give the friend group of Jungle Brothers, Tribe Called Quest, and De La Soul. They sought something they could shout out on records, to demonstrate common purpose and spirit. The idea was inspired by P-Funk, where there's an umbrella group name with numerous spin-offs.

"African Cry" is a variation on John D. Loudermilk's song "Indian Reservation (The Lament of the Cherokee Reservation Indian)," which Paul Revere & the Raiders hit #1 with in 1971. New Birth, a funk group from Detroit with roots in Louisville, updated it to be Afrocentric, retaining the lyric "They took away our native tongue." In Q-Tip's telling of the story, in the documentary *Beats, Rhymes & Life*, he said the lyric kept sticking in his head. "Native tongue" spoke to having a shared identity and language. From first hearing each other's music to having the sort of studio "sleepovers" that led to "Buddy," they felt like they were with kindred spirits.

The remix "Buddy (Native Tongues Decision)" is the definitive Native Tongues song, the only track to feature everyone considered to be part of Native Tongues from the start. The idea to do a remix came from the way De La Soul and Jungle Brothers were performing "Buddy" live, using the beat of Taana Gardner's "Heartbeat." Doing it this way was Q-Tip's idea, per a *HipHopDX* interview with Mase. Pos started working on a studio version of the remix and then got everyone else involved to record new versions of their vocals ("same vocals, but fresh," Mase said). They invited three more artists to Calliope Studios who ended up appearing on the track: Queen Latifah, Monie Love, and Phife Dawg.

Queen Latifah, born Dana Owens, was a fellow Tommy Boy artist. De La Soul were sitting in the label's office when

Monica Lynch and Dante Ross listened to Queen Latifah's demo tape for the first time. Throughout 1989 she was working toward the release of her debut album *All Hail the Queen*, released in November. On the "Buddy" remix she doesn't rap, but sings some lines based on "O-o-h Child" by the Five Stairsteps.

Monie Love, born Simone Gooden, was from the UK, part of a growing hip-hop scene in London. When she was sixteen, she met and befriended the Jungle Brothers and Queen Latifah through writer Dave "Funken" Klein, when they were touring the UK. After she was signed to a label (Chrysalis UK), and Afrika Baby Bam was chosen to produce her debut album, she met everyone.

Phife, born Malik Taylor, was Q-Tip's rhyming partner in A Tribe Called Quest. Phife and Q-Tip met and became friends at age four, and it was Phife who pushed his friend to start rapping. Though Q-Tip had mentioned Tribe in his appearances on the Jungle Brothers songs, the group didn't have any recordings yet, just a demo tape they were shopping to labels. The "Buddy" remix was the first released song that Phife rapped on.

The remix was the version used for the "Buddy" music video. Everybody on the track, and many of their friends, were at the video shoot. Pos also invited dancers he'd seen at clubs. Jeff, from the De La B-sides, is standing next to the young rapper Chi-Ali in the video. Red Alert is in the crowd. Phife is visible, but unfortunately his verse was dropped to shorten the length—the remix is over eight minutes long. The video begins with a perfectly absurdist Prince Paul moment. He walks along a brick wall, sets down a boom box and presses Play, so we can hear his voice explain the definition of "buddy" while he stands silently by.

The Native Tongues is thought of by fans, and written about by critics, as a collective or even a movement. It represented Afrocentric living, creative freedom, and nonconformity, within the genre and beyond. The legacy of that Native Tongues sound and approach has been felt in hip-hop ever since.

To De La Soul, Native Tongues was just friends hanging out. "It was the best thing that never happened," Maseo likes to say in interviews. All three members of De La have at various times told interviewers that the Native Tongues was just the one song, the "Buddy" remix, and friends hanging out together. It could have been something bigger or more official, but never was. It also could have involved different artists, depending on who was around for which session at what point. Who appeared on which songs by which artists was more happenstance than planning. Monie Love told the *People's Party with Talib Kweli* podcast that the studio sessions were "just vibes," informally being around like-minded artists, and that any friend was invited to any of the sessions, especially De La's.

To listeners, Native Tongues is an era and a concept, and has its own discography—both the individual efforts by each artist and those where they directly collaborated. The heart of that collaborative era would be the first few years, 1989–1992 (extending somewhat to include '88 and '93). In 1989, along with *3 Feet High and Rising* and the "Buddy" remix, came the Jungle Brothers' *Done by the Forces of Nature* and Queen Latifah's *All Hail the Queen*. Both featured collaborative Native Tongues songs.

The JBs had the 1990 single "Doin' Our Own Dang," the closest thing to a "Buddy" sequel. It followed the "Buddy" pattern of having an album version, but then a remix that was used for the video. Rapping on the album version were (in order): Maseo ("the one they call Baby Huey / the one that gets all the buddy"), Mike G, Q-Tip, Posdnuos, Monie Love, Afrika, Mike G (again), and Trugoy. Queen Latifah speaks part of the chorus. In the video/remix version, the last two verses, by Mike G and Trugoy, were cut.

Q-Tip's verse speaks to their collective pursuit of artistic growth, in an idealistic fashion: "A tree is growing / can't you see what I see?" Trugoy tries to make it clear it's not about setting a template for everyone to follow ("Don't follow the path that we're stepping"), but encouraging individual expression within a creative family: "Let the groove of the new proceed."

The cover photo for the twelve-inch single has become a commonly used image to represent the Native Tongues. It was taken by the British photographer Janette Beckman and orchestrated by Chris Lighty, the Jungle Brothers road manager at the time, and an employee at Rush Artist Management. (In 1996, Lighty would start his Violator Management company and soon become an influential figure in the business side of the industry, making a huge impact on the mainstream globalization of hip-hop.)

In the photo, nine people are laughing while they play around with musical instruments. All three Jungle Brothers are there, plus Q-Tip, Ali Shaheed Muhammad, Monie Love, Posdnuos, Mase, and Chris Lighty (a.k.a. Baby Chris). Where's Trugoy? He got bored doing the photo shoot and went home.

Queen Latifah's *All Hail the Queen* featured Monie Love on the feminist anthem "Ladies First." The album's second song had Native Tongues vibes, with De La Soul as guests. "Mama Gave Birth to the Soul Children" was produced by

Prince Paul and featured De La as Latifah's "soul children." It's the outro of the song that evokes the Native Tongues most, with Pos and Trugoy giving shout-outs in *Chipmunks*-style manipulated voices. They say hi to Mase, to the Jungle Brothers, to Q-Tip and Ali "from Quest," to Queen Latifah's crew the Flavor Unit and dancers the Safari Sisters, to Afrika Bambaataa, DJ Red Alert, and Prince Paul ("Yeah, the dew doo man!"). They ask Latifah, "Mommy, is the tribe really that big?" Her answer: "The tribe is as big as the ocean."

There were other songs with individual guest features, usually because someone happened to be at a studio session. In 1993, Trugoy did the hook on A Tribe Called Quest's classic "Award Tour," interpolating the melody of Malcolm McLaren and the World's Famous Supreme Team's "Hobo Scratch" ("We're on a world tour with Mr. Malcolm McLaren"). And there were other less prominent songs that featured some of the groups together. Two De La Soul B-sides featured Tribe: 1994's "Sh. Fe. MC's" and 1991's "What Yo Life Can Truly Be," which also had Black Sheep on it.

The song that came closest to being an iconic Native Tongues posse cut was A Tribe Called Quest's "Scenario," off their second album, 1991's *The Low End Theory*. It went through multiple variations before landing on the classic Tribe / Leaders of the New School combination. The first version included Pos, Black Sheep, and "Baby Chris" Lighty. In an interview with *Unkut*, the Public Enemy–affiliated DJ Johnny Juice described being at the recording session for one of the early, unreleased versions: "Everybody rhymed on it but Q-Tip, and the best motherfucker on that shit was Posdnuos. He fuckin' destroyed it, and he ain't even like the beat!" In interviews Posdnuos has affirmed that he wasn't a fan of his verse, or the version of the song that he was on. The final version of "Scenario," the Tribe/Leaders version, may not have a cohesive "Native Tongues" lineup (no De La or Jungle Brothers), but it was an instant classic that hastened Busta Rhymes' emergence as a solo star.

The ambiguity about who was or wasn't part of the Native Tongues set fans up for debating it forever. Even the groups themselves, if asked by interviewers, will give different answers. Some will mention adjacent artists that guested on individual songs by Tribe or De La, or were hanging around with the same friend group at the time: Leaders of the New School, Brand Nubian, KMD, the Beatnuts (especially JuJu), Fu-Schnickens, Da Bush Babees. One could include the supporting musicians or studio technicians who were involved in multiple Native Tongues projects: studio engineer Bob Power and singer Vinia Mojica, for example. There are legions of artists clearly influenced by the original groups that a case could be made for, including those who collaborated with De La or Tribe later: Common, Mos Def (now known as Yasiin Bey), Talib Kweli. There were also at least two subgroups within Native Tongues that never yielded recordings: Kids on Zenith Ave (Dave, Mase, Mike G, and Jarobi of A Tribe Called Quest) and the Fabulous Fleas (Pos, Q-Tip, Afrika Baby Bam, and JuJu).

Two others "officially" became new Native Tongues acts, because one of the core groups started referring to them as such. Black Sheep, the duo of Dres and Mista Lawnge, were present for De La Soul's sessions for their second album (*De La Soul Is Dead*), and possibly earlier. In the book *Check the Technique: Volume 2*, Lawnge said he did some of the scratches on "Buddy," uncredited. They released their own debut album, *A Wolf in Sheep's Clothing*, in 1991, with the hit "The Choice Is Yours." They named their group in relation to Native Tongues, as if they were the "black sheep" of the family.

The young rapper Chi Ali was just fifteen when he made his rhyming debut on the Black Sheep album. When he released his LP *The Fabulous Chi Ali*, recorded at Calliope Studios, produced largely by the Beatnuts and with Trugoy guesting on two songs, it included another track in the lineage of Native Tongues posse cuts: "Let the Horns Blow" featuring Dres, Trugoy, Phife Dawg, and Fashion (a.k.a. Al' Tariq, one of the founding members of the Beatnuts).

There's a leaked Tribe demo recording of Q-Tip doing a song called "In Native Tongue." References to the JBs' first album and to "all the Natives" would put it somewhere in the 1988–89 era, before Tribe signed a deal but likely after the "Native Tongues" idea emerged. DJ Shadow owns the demo tape, as part of his personal collection of four hundred to five hundred rap demo tapes. He played the song on a 2016 BBC mix and told *Stereogum* it's from Tribe's first demo. The song ends, "You must be Native to possess the true tongue."

In a 2018 interview with CNBC's Jon Fortt for his *Fortt Knox* podcast, Q-Tip described Native Tongues as allowing for "different shades of black complexity," adding, "we were able to express that we were more than one dimension." Even if the Native Tongues consisted of just one song, or was more a concept, it meant much more to listeners. The loose group of artists and performers was uniquely influential for generations of musicians, to this day, even in genres beyond hip-hop.

6. TRYING TO STILL LIVE: CONTROLLING THE NARRATIVE THROUGH *DE LA SOUL IS DEAD*

In 2014, John Oates told the *Philadelphia Inquirer* that Hall & Oates' "I Can't Go for That (No Can Do)" was about more than it seemed: "The song is really about not being pushed around by big labels, managers, and agents and being told what to do, and being true to yourself creatively." The spirit of artistic independence that runs through *3 Feet High and Rising* is thus built into the album's very DNA. Present at the building-block level are stories of the struggle between art and commerce, the legacy of corporations trying to harness others' artistic output and channel it for their own financial gain.

The commercial and critical reaction to *3 Feet High and Rising* brought success to De La Soul and Tommy Boy, but it also brought unexpected attention that heightened tensions between the two. The newness of De La Soul's approach to sampling—the quantity of samples they used and the variety of sources—was not something Tommy Boy was prepared for. Their approach to legal clearances was to clear the most prominent and obvious samples, but not those used more minimally within a song, or by more obscure artists. For example, Tommy Boy made agreements with Steely Dan for using "Peg" in "Eye Know," and with Hall & Oates for using "I Can't Go for That" in "Say No Go." Per a 1989 *Spin* article, George Clinton's deal for the use of "Not Just Knee Deep" in "Me Myself and I" gave him one cent per album sold and one and two-thirds cents per single sold, plus half the publishing royalties. (Clinton himself wrote in his memoir that Tommy Boy paid him $100,000.)

The *3 Feet* track "Transmitting Live from Mars" included a sample of the Turtles that fell into the minimal, inconspicuous-use category. One minute and twelve seconds, "Transmitting Live" is more like a segue, a lead-in to "Eye Know." Voices from a French-language instruction record ask what time it is ("Quelle heure est-il?") and talk about lunch over a loop of an organ and drums from Wilson Pickett's 1969 cover of "Hey Jude." Then there is a looped twelve-second bit from the Turtles' "You Showed Me," the keyboard notes and strings that begin the song.

The song "You Showed Me" was written by Gene Clark and James Roger McGuinn before they formed the Byrds. The Turtles' 1968 version was their last US hit, reaching #6 on the singles chart. The track was attributed to Nature's Children on the concept album *The Turtles Present the Battle of the Bands*, where each song was given a fictitious band name. When the Turtles broke up two years later, members Mark Volman and Howard Kaylan continued as a duo. First, they were part of Frank Zappa's band under the name Phlorescent Leech & Eddie, and then Flo & Eddie.

As the story goes, in 1989 one of the two former Turtles heard his daughter listening to *3 Feet High and Rising* and recognized the bit from "You Showed Me." Kaylan and Volman filed a lawsuit in US District Court against De La Soul, Prince Paul, and Tommy Boy for $1.7 million in punitive damages. In *Spin*, Turtles lawyer Evan Cohen said before filing the suit he approached Tommy Boy and they offered a flat fee of $1,000, what they would have expected to pay had they made an agreement ahead of time.

According to Posdnuos in *The Hip Hop Years*, the Turtles told the group they would drop the lawsuit if De La Soul agreed to play on the next Flo & Eddie / Turtles album. De La Soul declined. The parties settled out of court for an undisclosed amount. De La Soul wasn't yet seeing much financial reward for the album's success; they also didn't see the financial impact of the settlement. It was something the label handled. Kayman's 2013 memoir depicts himself and Volman as saviors that allowed all musicians after them to get paid: "No one who had ever been sampled had the balls to say anything about it . . . we set the new standard."

The Turtles lawsuit was the biggest and most public, but it was not the only lawsuit or complaint against De La Soul for samples on *3 Feet*. The others were quietly handled by the label (for example, Monica Lynch has made reference to a cease-and-desist letter from Steely Dan, upon the album's release, that was settled). Yet the legal hassles had less of an impact creatively on De La Soul's next album than the overall media portrayal of the group as hippies.

In the period before their second album was released, media reports emerged that De La Soul was finished. They weren't going to make any more music; they were going to open a donut shop or a record store. Or they were starting their own radio station. That news turned into mentions of a new album. In a 1990 *Toronto Star* article, Trugoy gave the working title as *Yeah, We Opened Up a Do-Nut Shop*. According to *Ego Trip* magazine, the original title of the album was *We Fell into a Bottle of Plastic Shwingalokate, So*

We Opened a Radio Station. That word "Shwingalokate" ended up being a song title. It was also mentioned in the *3 Feet* liner notes, at the end of a shout-out to the Native Tongues: "Preparation for Shwingalokate has now begun. We must prepare the listeners for its coming."

The donut shop and radio station themes did remain within the album. But the actual title they landed on added both weight and the connotation of stark change. It started as a joke that Trugoy made about the strains of their touring schedule. The group was looking at a Rush Artist Management whiteboard that listed their upcoming tour dates. Feeling overscheduled and burned-out, Trugoy wiped away the dates below the group name and replaced them with the words "Is Dead." It drew laughs but also sparked Posdnuos's imagination.

The title *De La Soul Is Dead* was decided on before they had a meaning for it and before the artwork and overall concept. They had been working on new songs in some capacity since before their debut was released. Posdnuos recalled to *NME* sitting in the studio with the Jungle Brothers, not long after *3 Feet High and Rising*'s release, feeling jealous because he wanted to work in the studio himself, to get started on the next De La album.

Tommy Boy increased the budget somewhat for *De La Soul Is Dead*, given the success of the first album. In the wake of the Turtles' lawsuit, the label also made more of an effort to clear samples. De La Soul did not consciously change their sampling approach because of the Turtles' lawsuit, but they made sure the label knew about, and cleared, every single sample. That led to higher costs for the album, from the sample clearances alone.

They recorded at the same studio as the first album,

Calliope, and used similar equipment. The album was mixed at Island Media, same as *3 Feet*. What had changed was the group's confidence level working with studio engineers and the equipment.

Prince Paul agreed to work on the album, but tried stepping back a bit, in deference to the trio. "I was trying to ween myself out of being the main production person," he told the *Smoking Section* in 2008. In the credits, Prince Paul is listed as co-producer with the group, versus producer on *3 Feet*. At this point Prince Paul was also still in Stetsasonic, but that group was winding down. They ended up releasing their third and then-final album, *Blood, Sweat & No Tears*, a few months before *De La Soul Is Dead*.

First single "Ring Ring Ring (Ha Ha Hey)" was released a few months before the LP, giving the impression of a more refined, sophisticated version of De La Soul, but still with an overriding sense of humor. The topic came from a real-life prank they would play on each other. If someone asked one of them for a phone number, they would instead give out the number of someone else in the group. In the song, they seemed to poke fun both at their success and at the increasing demands of others to help them out in the music business. A mark of success is how many more people expect something from you.

The music came from Pos's idea to emulate the chorus of the British pop group Curiosity Killed the Cat's 1989 song "Name and Number" ("Hey, how ya doin', I'm sorry you couldn't get through / 'Cause this is a message that's been recorded especially for you / and if you leave a name and your number, we'll get right back to you"), put it over the music to "Help Is on the Way" by the Whatnauts (a soul single from 1981), and make the song be about aspiring rappers giving them their demo tapes. The "Help Is on the Way" guitar part is a continual loop in the song, the earworm melody. In the original it is more like a recurring melody in the background.

Prince Paul originally made the beat—built off "God Made Me Funky" by the Headhunters—for Mikey D, the Queens rapper who gave LL Cool J his stage name and later replaced Large Professor in Main Source. He had also given it to Puff Daddy as an option for Heavy D. Neither were happening, so he gave it to De La for "Ring Ring Ring." Paul has said that Puff and Heavy D became upset with him, when they decided they wanted to use it. They would end up using it anyway, for a remix of a song by Soul for Real featuring Heavy D. ("He just would not get denied," Paul told *What Had Happened Was*.)

The twelve-inch single included a flute-riddled remix ("Piles and Piles of Demo Tapes Bi-Da Miles (Conley's Decision)," featuring Pic "Supercat" Conley on flute) that now feels like an introduction to the nineties' De La Soul era *and* future-oriented, carrying the secret knowledge that three decades later one of the group's bohemian spawn, André 3000 of Outkast, would set down the mic and pick up a flute.

The black-and-white "Ring Ring Ring" video, directed by Mark Romanek, presented a different image of the group right away. Gone were the Day-Glo colors; their haircuts were trimmed down. The music had a sort of tasteful jazz angle to it, the dancers in the video had a Black-bohemian look. The video starts with Trugoy woken up by an answering machine message and rolling his eyes. At the end of the video, a pot of daisies falls to the ground. A crashed pot of daisies was on the album cover as well, based on a sketch by

Joe Buck (Joseph Buckingham), whom De La Soul knew from the flyers he drew for college parties at the New York Institute of Technology in Islip, Long Island. Visually and symbolically, the D.A.I.S.Y. Age was over.

De La Soul Is Dead was released on May 14, 1991, the same day as KMD's *Mr. Hood* and Ice-T's *O.G. Original Gangster*. From one angle, the album came from a similar place as *3 Feet High and Rising*. There are juvenile jokes (about body odor and name-calling) and De La speak. There are new slang words and a running joke where they say a nonsense phrase that sounds like "ahigahigeehigee," and then a sample of Slick Rick intoning, "I can't be your lover," from "La Di Da Di." They again sample from a diverse array of sources—taking records from across decades and eras and utilizing them within the De La universe for texture, melody, and groove, or as punch lines.

The first proper track "Oodles of O's" uses the bass line from Tom Waits's "Diamonds on My Windshield," which reflected the loneliness and motion of highway driving in the 1974 original. In De La Soul's hands, over drums from Lafayette Afro Rock Band ("Hihache," 1973) the bass line's meandering qualities feel strange, almost mystical, like we're winding our way into a tunnel or a portal to another dimension.

Across the album, the samples are as varied as on their debut, yet heavier on the seventies. Some prominent obscure ones include the funk band Slave ("Just a Touch of Love," on "Keepin' the Faith"), two Serge Gainsbourg songs (horns from "Les Oubliettes" on "Talkin' bout Hey Love" and a groove from "En Melody" on "Not Over till the Fat Lady Plays the Demo"), and Busta "Cherry" Jones's bluesy duo White Lightnin' ("That's No Lie" on "Fanatic of the

B Word"). Though the group's layered approach to using samples is at times similar to their debut, there are no songs on *De La Soul Is Dead* where the sample count climbs as high into the double digits as it did on the *3 Feet* collage "Cool Breeze on the Rocks," or even sections of "The Magic Number."

The album is filled with bitterness. The humor has turned dark, and the list of people they have issues with seems ever-growing. The group's targets include: anyone who thinks they're soft or can't fight, listeners or interviewers who think they're hippies, R&B singers, Black radio stations, men trying to act tougher than they are, women who won't have sex with them. Oh, and Arsenio Hall . . . who gets mocked on four tracks because of his "hippies of hip-hop" comment, including one where they imitate his "Let's get busy" catchphrase.

De La Soul Is Dead is like a concept album riddled with competing and intersecting concepts. It is a parody of a children's fable. It is a radio station that embodies the stereotypes of the day, from shout-out shows to a quiet-storm hour. It is a sophisticated soul/jazz-tinged record making fun of trendiness in music. It is a "donut-themed" album where the donuts represent anything circular: records, punches thrown in a fistfight, the sound of the letter *O* when voiced aloud.

"Pease Porridge" uses a children's song format to capture De La Soul's reaction to being considered peace-loving hippies who couldn't stand up for themselves in a fight. "Pease Porridge" is the musical version of De La Soul defending themselves physically on the Nitro tour. The song takes the children's fable imagery, via samples of the 1974 children's record *Rhythm and Rhyme: Activities for*

Early Childhood by Sharron Lucky, and juxtaposes it with rhymes about fighting. Along the way Kermit the Frog gets spoofed (Jarobi from Tribe mimics Kermit's voice), women gossip about a De La streetfight ("But I thought it was supposed to be about peace signs?"), Mikey Roads (their road manager Mike Jolicoeur) and Squirrel (road manager Miguel Muñoz) narrate a fight like they're sports analysts, and Trugoy rhymes, in a unique repeated-word style, "We bring we bring, we bring, we bring the peace of course / But pack a nine inside inside my De La drawers."

The six skits, spread across the album, came together after the songs, and were something they created in the moment, without a script. Prince Paul says he encouraged the skits to lighten up the tone of the album, which was getting dark as the group worked through their grievances. The conceit of the skits is a De La Soul read-along storybook, with chime noises when the listener is supposed to turn the page. The liner notes include comics spelling out the same story. Jeff, of the *3 Feet High and Rising* B-sides, finds a De La Soul tape in the garbage, and is beat up by a bully named Hemorrhoid, voiced by Mista Lawnge of Black Sheep, who calls him the worst insult, "Arsenio." Throughout the album they listen to the tape, hate it, beat up anybody who starts saying anything positive (with the smacking sounds of comic book story records). At the end they leave dissatisfied: "What happened to the pimps . . . the guns . . . the curse words . . . that's what rap music is all about, right?"

Mocking rap stereotypes is a *De La Soul Is Dead* pastime. De La Soul put a harder musical edge on their songs whenever they mock emcees trying to be hard, part of their perpetual aptitude, intentional or not, for leaving listeners confused. An example of this is "Afro Connections at a Hi

5 (In the Eyes of a Hoodlum)," where their emulations of rappers trying to be hard spiral out in a detailed direction—from how they fight and present themselves ("Now I hold my crotch cause I'm top-notch") to what they eat and how many pairs of jeans are in their closet (thirteen). Mase's multiple vocal appearances on the album add a dual sense of hardness and humor, especially when he raps in a funky, loose manner on "Let, Let Me In" and "Afro Connections." ("Afro" is one of the songs on the album that Mase produced, along with "Keepin' the Faith" and "Shwingalokate.")

Four of the album's songs are only present on the CD version—not the cassette or vinyl—based on how much music could fit comfortably on what format at the time. In their humor, a few of those songs exemplify the fine line between skit and song. That includes the pseudo-cocktail lounge number "Johnny's Dead aka Vincent Mason (Live from the BK Lounge)," where Trugoy sounds almost Dylan-like or country & western-ish as he seemingly improvises his way through a few lines about Johnny having a bullet in his head.

"Kicked out the House" makes fun of the trend of mixing hip-hop with house music ("hip house"), while doubling down on the "I can't be your lover" sample. The strangest of the CD-only songs is "Who Do U Worship?," a nihilistic exercise that shifts back and forth from gentle to extreme. That is, from acoustic guitar, a replayed imitation of a José Feliciano sample that got too expensive to use, to screaming intermixed with some indistinguishable rock samples. The vocals sarcastically voice the perspective of someone evil: "Damn, I feel good today. I look forward to going in and just beating the shit out of somebody and taking their money."

The radio station theme and the voices within the songs

that comment on the songs themselves make *De La Soul Is Dead* an album about music and the act of engaging with it. Multiple songs begin as if someone has just tuned into a radio station. "Talkin' bout Hey Love" sounds for its first minute and a half like Posdnuos is speaking lyrics that a female singer (Ann Roberts) is singing, as if he's rhyming along with a song he's hearing on the radio. The use of "Hey Love" by Stevie Wonder, from 1966, presents another dimension. Posdnuos is rhyming along with a song where a female singer is singing about asking a DJ at a club to play the song that she's singing about, or perhaps the song she's in.

The meta-title "A Roller Skating Jam Named 'Saturdays'" does something similar. The title itself is as if a radio DJ is announcing the next song: "Here for you is a roller-skating jam, named 'Saturdays.'" And it starts that way, with Russell Simmons as a WRMS DJ introducing the track. Then the song is exactly as advertised, a retro roller-rink jam, sort of serious and very not. The music is built off "Evil Vibrations" by Mighty Ryeders, plus Tower of Power drums and some snippets of other seventies summer jams. The presence of a "Saturday in the Park" sample makes it seem like that song by Chicago *is* the roller-skating jam; this may be another song about listening to a song.

Vinia Mojica sings the chorus, and per a 2012 interview with *The Revivalist*, she was asked to sing in an ironic way. "I'm glad people like it, but it's not really me," she said, though it's one of the tracks she's most recognized for. Originally the song was not envisioned to have her vocals. The idea was to have Posdnuos and Trugoy rhyme a chorus, in a style based off the vocals of Chic's "Good Times." The track was first created by Posdnuos not for De La Soul, but for the Native Tongues side group the Fabulous Fleas. When

Tommy Boy wanted a song that sounded like it could be a hit single, Pos redirected it to De La Soul. Q-Tip, one of the Fabulous Fleas, is on "Saturdays," rapping the first verse. Released as the second single, the song was somewhat of a dance club hit, one of three De La Soul songs to chart in the Top 10 on *Billboard*'s Dance Club Songs chart (along with "Say No Go" and "Me Myself and I," which hit #1).

Through the album's meta radio theme, De La Soul also gets the chance to make fun of the conventions of the day—and, by relation, the entire industry built around selling and promoting music. There's a slow-jam radio segue, where the slow-as-molasses DJ declares that WRMS plays nothing but "De La Slow" music. "Rap de Rap Show" satirizes radio show call-in shout-outs. Q-Tip, De La Soul, the Jungle Brothers, and others phone in to shout out their favorite DJ, the Dew Doo Man (a.k.a. Prince Paul). This gives Prince Paul the opportunity to yell, "Who's the Dew Doo Man?" and have a crowd respond, "You're the Dew Doo Man!"

Even a song like "Oodles of O's" has something meta and literal about it. It's a song about how many "o" sounds are voiced in the song itself ("bro," "glow," "embryo," etc.). The track was originally created for Run-D.M.C., when they were soliciting beats for one of their nineties "comeback" albums. Run-D.M.C. rejected it, and apparently not in a gracious manner. It's a safe bet that De La Soul used it to more unique ends.

De La Soul Is Dead is multisided in just about every way. There are multiple concepts entwined, multiple running jokes, multiple targets of their bitter humor. They use the voices of themselves and other people in a complex way. On both "Talkin' bout Hey Love" and "Bitties in the BK Lounge," partway through the song a woman takes a central role to spar with one of the men. On "Hey Love," it's not the same woman who is singing but Tesha Sills who banters back and forth with Pos about their relationship.

"Bitties in the BK Lounge" takes a humorous look at fans' interactions with celebrities out in public, inspired by real experiences they had on tour (including one at a Burger King in Lawrence, Kansas). It also recalls the fact that all three members of De La Soul worked at Burger King as teenagers (Mase worked at a BK by a bowling alley, the other two at the BK in the mall). The back-and-forth between Pos and the character of Shashawna on "Bitties" is like a sillier fast-food version of Ice Cube versus Yo-Yo on "It's a Man's World" or Too Short and Rappin' 4-Tay versus Danger Zone (Barbie and Entice) on "Don't Fight the Feelin'." And just as much a precursor for later male-female argument songs with a darker side like "Domestic Violence" by RZA as Bobby Digital and Kendrick Lamar featuring Taylour Paige's "We Cry Together."

The female rapper on "Bitties" going toe-to-toe with Pos is credited in the liner notes as Almond Joy. Le'Shaun Denine Toureau met De La Soul through the Jungle Brothers, and was part of the crowd of friends that would hang out and party together. A rapper who released two singles through Tommy Boy in the early nineties, she had somewhat of a hit back in high school with the track "Wild Thang" by her duo 2 Much (1988). It's the song LL Cool J remade for his Top 10 hit "Doin' It," featuring Le'Shaun herself on vocals. She's also on Monie Love's 1990 single "Monie in the Middle," and has said she probably appears somewhere in the background on other Native Tongues–related songs, from being in the studio. In 2023 she told the podcast *Halftime Chat* she can't even remember if she got paid for being on

"Bitties." At the time, it was more about hanging out with friends: showing up at each other's recording sessions, eating Chinese food, and contributing to records on the fly. Her last line in "Bitties," "I think I'll go get me some Chinese food," could be literal. She might have gotten off the mic and walked across the room to get something to eat.

The crowd of voices on De La Soul's first two albums came directly from the group's habit of inviting friends to the studio to hang out. On *De La Soul Is Dead* the crowd makes for a complex array of voices within the songs. There are the women on "Bitties," the voices calling in to the "Rap de Rap Show," the sing-along chorus of voices on "Fanatic of the B Word" (which also has guest bits from Mike G and a verse from Dres), the various sampled voices on "Pass the Plugs" (Prince Paul's voice sampled from "Description" and "Double Huey Skit," and even the voice of Gangster "B" from "Cold Waxin' the Party"), and the crowd yelling out on "Shwingalokate," which also has Daddy-O singing part of the hook (the track was originally meant for Stetsasonic). The album's variety of intermingled voices and textures grew from what they did on *3 Feet*, yet also feels like a one-of-a-kind achievement, especially when combined with the multiple concepts and continued use of diverse samples. The album is a multiverse.

De La Soul Is Dead was not just about the group's beefs with the world. "Millie Pulled a Pistol on Santa" is an exemplary story-song, transferring their concern for social issues into a dynamic narrative. The song title was something Pos wrote down as an idea in his notebook after seeing a homeless man in a subway station wearing a dirty Santa outfit. The topic and story for the song came later. Pos knew someone in an abusive family situation, with their father; thinking about it, he decided to connect the emotions and experience of that story to the "Santa" title. "I was really upset about that and just applied it to wax," he told *Spin* in 1991. The music and the full picture of the song came a few months later, hearing beats Prince Paul had sent for consideration. Pos told *GQ* that the music sounded "eerie and sad . . . that's when the journey of writing the story started."

That music represents another use of classic Funkadelic material. The song starts with the spoken intro from "Mommy, What's a Funkadelic?" ("If you will suck my soul, I will lick your funky emotions") before shifting into a track built around "I'll Stay." "Eerie and sad" sums up "I'll Stay" well. Eddie Hazel's guitar is tender, like it's filled with regret.

One of the songs only available on the CD version, "My Brother's a Basehead" is another song Posdnuos drew from tough personal experiences: an older brother, Tyrone, who was struggling with crack addiction. The song was born of hurt and anger. There's an almost sitcom-like quality to it, from the tone of the intro ("This particular element . . . is me, brotha!") to the jaunty, would-be TV-theme music built off a sample of sixties songs (the Doors' "Touch Me," "Game of Love" by Wayne Fontana & the Mindbenders, "Hang on Sloopy" by the McCoys). But Posdnuos's rhymes aren't humorous, stepping through a story of brothers growing up; one brother follows his curiosity about drugs through to addiction. Pos describes the pull of addiction ("Said there was a voice inside you that talked / that said you shouldn't stop"). Trugoy's verse is from the perspective of the dealer. Pos pulls no punches in how he feels on the song: "Brother, brother, stupid brother of mine." A preacher and choir come in to give forgiveness, profess that his brother can still be saved. His brother is trying to walk the right path, with the church's help, but Pos is seeing through it ("Bullshit, didn't believe a lick / knew this fool too well for that to stick"). And it doesn't stick. The song has no big moment of redemption at the end; the title is present tense.

The De La Soul–curated issue of *Frank151* includes Pos interviewing his brother about the song and the experiences that drove it. Tyrone shares how he went from weed to cocaine to crack, and eventually to rehab, while Posdnuos describes the stress it put on their family. They talk about how similar they look to each other, and how that caused mistaken identity issues for them both. Pos admits that his writing and releasing "My Brother's a Basehead" came out of hurt, exasperation with the situation, and "a growing hate": "it was very spiteful . . . I knew it would hurt him."

In a *What Had Happened Was* episode, Prince Paul told Open Mike Eagle, "After recording the album, I remember telling the guys, 'This is a very mean album.'" And some critics and listeners did indeed take it that way.

Within the world of hip-hop, many understood what the group was doing on *De La Soul Is Dead*, in killing off the "hippie" imagery. In *The Source*'s 5 Mic review (actually 5 Records, before they switched the review-rating symbol from a record to a mic), the album was treated as a reaction to the hype, to get listeners focused on the music: "It should put the De La Hippie stuff to rest—for good."

Among music critics in general, the reactions varied. Simon Reynolds of *Melody Maker* admired the "more complicated and interesting" tension between optimism and cynicism. He started his review, "De La Soul may not be dead, but positivity smells kinda funny." In *Musician*, J.D. Considine saw the album as idealistic, sly, and more similar to the first than the angry satire implied. He wrote, "If *De La Soul Is Dead* was conceived as a means of undoing their hip-hop hippie image, it certainly has an odd way of going about it." In contrast, Jon Pareles in the *New York Times* was frustrated, even angry, with what he saw as the group being overly defensive and bitter about the fact that they got popular. The headline read, "Is De La Soul Dead or Just Too Famous?"

The pot of daisies crashing to the ground remains the image and idea associated with the album and this era of the group's music. To De La Soul, the image represented change, how a caterpillar will die and become a butterfly. As they told *The Vine* in 2011, it's as if familiar people "went through a metamorphosis and changed into these new three guys, who were a little bit older, but who were trying to still live and give you good music."

Later in their career, they would look back at this move as a lesson in "the importance of controlling the narrative." Maseo told the *Guardian* in 2023, "A hit record can hurt your entire body of work if you let the industry control your narrative." It was a pivotal moment in their career overall, when they took a stance of creative independence, of taking their music in the direction they wanted it to go. Questlove told Red Bull Music Academy he sees *De La Soul Is Dead* as the group's reaction to realizing their audience was whiter than they had planned: "You think you're doing a Black art form . . . and a whole 'nother culture gravitates towards it."

The album was a clear attempt to take a firm grasp on their career and the narrative around it. Did it work? Posdnuos jokingly told *Rolling Stone* that the flowers at photo shoots soon got replaced by caskets.

Per *Spin*, Prince Paul let the group turn down his more

pop-oriented ideas for *De La Soul Is Dead*. "This time it was more of an art thing." Around this same time, he was trying to get his own projects going. After the success of *3 Feet*, and the Prince Paul–produced "The Gas Face" by 3rd Bass (ft. Zev Love X of KMD), Prince Paul was approached by Russell Simmons and Lyor Cohen about starting his own label, as an imprint within Rush Associated Labels (RAL), the umbrella company they created to handle Def Jam and their other labels. After declining a few times, he agreed and signed a deal. He named it Dew Doo Man Records, with a logo that looks a lot like the poop emoji.

Dew Doo Man Records never came to be. Although Prince Paul was told he could do whatever he wanted creatively, when he would bring demos to Simmons and Cohen, they were unimpressed. The artists Prince Paul started with for the label were Mic Teluxe (Mike Teelucksingh) and Resident Alien (a trio of Double Brain, Dragon, and Mr. Bug). There's a Resident Alien album called *It Takes a Nation of Suckas to Let Us In* that almost made it to release in 1991. There was one single ("Mr. Boops"), and a video for the song "Ooh the Doo Dew Man," which serves as an introductory theme for the label. But Simmons wasn't happy with the lack of a clear hit; he and Prince Paul agreed to dismantle the label agreement before anything was released.

7. THROUGH THE MACHINE: *BUHLOONE MINDSTATE* AND GROWING UP

By the time of their third album, 1993's *Buhloone Mindstate*, De La Soul were in a different place in their personal lives and professional careers. They had children. They owned houses. They had families to support. Their creative adventure had turned into a business, a livelihood. It had been that way since the unexpected success of *3 Feet High and Rising*, but now it was especially so.

To *A.V. Club* in 2000 Posdnuos described this as a "peaceful period" in the life of De La Soul; they had come to terms with their place in music, with their past. They were no longer reacting to the success of their debut or to the media and audience profiling of the group. "We felt confident knowing we weren't going to change for anyone," he said. He has often stressed what he hears as the relaxed, calm atmosphere of the resulting album. Hot 97's *Ebro in the Morning* called *Buhloone Mindstate* "a calm quiet album amongst organized noise."

Jolicoeur has described the period and the album differently; he was not in a peaceful mindset. He was burnt out and frustrated by the group's experiences within the music industry. As he phrased it to Oliver Wang during interviews for an NPR story on the album's twentieth anniversary, they had "been through the machine." Jolicoeur wasn't even sure about doing another album. He was tired of trying to keep up with record label and media expectations. Tommy Boy was still looking for the trio to repeat the success of "Me Myself and I" and *3 Feet High and Rising*. Trugoy started officially going by his first name of Dave as his artist name, his way of expressing frustration with the industry. He also started covering up his eye in photos and videos, a counter to how he used his eye to indicate "I" in the video for "Me Myself and I." It more likely references the *Buhloone* song "Eye Patch"—"mess up my mind with the eye patch"—and its third-eye connotations.

The group recorded at a few different NYC studios: Sorcerer Sound, Magic Shop, Platinum Island, and River Sound. All three members also had their own home studios. The preproduction work was in a more polished state than in the early days of pause tapes and Casio samplers. Per Maseo in a 2017 interview on the *Sucka Free Stogie Show* podcast, each of them was "bringing a track to the table instead of a skeleton."

The label was still eager for a hit song, but they also mostly let De La Soul follow their own musical path. The resulting album had its own sound that eschewed some of the qualities that marked the first two albums. Gone were the zany skits, the abrupt detours into set pieces mid-song, the discernable crowd of on-the-fly collaborators, and the layers of samples.

Hip-hop as a whole had changed the trajectory of its sample use since De La Soul's previous album. *Paul's Boutique, Fear of a Black Planet*, and *De La Soul Is Dead* ended up being a crescendo of that approach that broke at the end of 1991. This was due to the results of a lawsuit that was even bigger in its scope and impact than the Turtles suit.

On Biz Markie's third album, *I Need a Haircut*, on the song "Alone Again" he used an overt sample of Gilbert O'Sullivan's "Alone Again (Naturally)" without permission (or after being outright denied), with Biz singing the title hook as the chorus. Biz Markie and his recording and production companies lost the subsequent court case, with the ruling that sampling without permission infringed against the original copyright owners. Sampling drastically changed after this decision. The cost of making records filled with dozens of layered samples became too much for most artists and their labels, so they sampled more selectively. (The name of Biz Markie's next album: *All Samples Cleared!*).

Going into the creation of *Buhloone Mindstate*, De La Soul knew they wanted something less sprawling than their first two LPs: no skits, fewer songs. Prince Paul was again involved in a production role. He was more hands-off, guiding and helping the trio more than steering the overall concept. He often had his baby son in the studio with him, in his arms or free to bang on the equipment. That son would grow up to be DJ PForReal, the touring DJ for Lil Uzi Vert.

During the time he was working with De La on *Buhloone*, Prince Paul was also shopping around a demo he had put together the year before, with a new group of artists who were disappointed with their individual experiences so far in the industry. Poetic (of Too Poetic), whom Paul knew from Long Island, had been dropped from Tommy Boy after one single. Prince Rakeem, now starting to go by the name RZA, also had a frustrating stint on Tommy Boy. Paul's Stetsasonic bandmate Frukwan had quit Stet before the third album. As a group, they were calling themselves the Gravediggaz.

Despite his more hands-off approach, much of the early crafting of the music for *Buhloone Mindstate* came from Prince Paul and Posdnuos working together, and then getting input from Mase, before pulling in Dave. The title concept of a balloon mind state came with the tagline, "It might blow up, but it won't go pop," a line from the song "Patti Dooke." Throughout the album are references, some clear and some elusive, toward success and its fragility, and the fine line between commercial success and failure.

The album was preceded by the single "Breakadawn," an attempt to appease the record label's desire for a hit. Around the time of *De La Soul Is Dead*, Posdnuos made the track for Mic Teluxe, one of the artists Prince Paul was working with for his Dew Doo Man label. When the label wanted another song to be the single, he repurposed the Mic Teluxe track. The title phrase comes from Smokey Robinson's voice, a sample from his song "Quiet Storm" (the song that lent its name to a whole subgenre). The bulk of the music and vibe of "Breakadawn" comes from Michael Jackson's "I Can't Help It." It was a song Pos always wanted to sample. He thought of combining the two while watching Smokey Robinson sing on a TV special celebrating Motown Records' twenty-fifth anniversary (*Motown 25: Yesterday, Today, Forever*).

Dave told *GQ* "Breakadawn" was one of his least favorite De La Soul songs and felt like a too intentional attempt for the group to sell records. It reflected all his uncertainties about the music industry and record label pressures influencing the art. "It almost felt like a slave record." He similarly told journalist Oliver Wang, it "was just a fluffy record to me . . . not what I wanted to begin representing with De La again. Shooting the video was the worst day of my life."

The "Breakadawn" video was directed by Mark Gerard, who the same year directed one for Apache's Q-Tip-produced "Gangsta Bitch." He has over a hundred music video credits to his name. The video feels like one of those composite photographs that show the same people multiple times. The trio wander around some kind of castle near a beach, and the camera is constantly either doubling them up or spinning around them. For all Dave's angst about the song and video, and worry that it was fluff, "Breakadawn" gave hints to their mindset on *Buhloone*. In the song there are multiple references to their biography, the hard work they put into touring, and the fragility of their success. Dave jokes about getting his WIC card ready, because "the days of the breaks are just about over."

Though she's not in the video, "Breakadawn" includes a few lines from the woman who served as almost an additional group member for the album: the young rapper Terressa Thompson, a.k.a. Shortie No Mass. She appears on the majority of songs, either rapping a few lines or echoing the others' voices.

Posdnuos brought her into the fold; he even gave her the rap name Shortie. They were introduced by his publicist at a concert in Philadelphia, and Pos invited her to come to NYC to visit. She ended up hanging out with De La Soul and friends, at a Black Sheep concert and in the studio. She told the Journalist Sin-Seer on his *The History Lesson* podcast that "it was surreal to be around people [she] idolized" like De La and Phife. During the *Buhloone* session, Pos told her she'd be a part of the album, even before he had heard her rhyme. He liked the way her voice sounded and thought it'd be cool to incorporate her into their sound. He later told *GQ*, "She was just like our little baby sister—hanging around and doing the parts she needed to do."

Pos wrote the majority of her rhymes, everything except her verse on one song ("In the Woods"), which she wrote. Her presence on the album presented an interesting shift to their sound. It's in keeping with their method from the start of integrating other people's voices, but it also made fans wonder if they were adding a fourth member, putting on a young artist they were going to be promoting, or what.

The album included songs produced by each member, and Prince Paul. They were again working with and adding to each other's ideas. One of Dave's few production contributions was the closing track, "Stone Age," featuring Biz Markie, someone he'd wanted to do a song with for a while. Biz also featured on one of the B-sides to the *Buhloone* single "Ego Trippin' (Part Two)," a track called "Lovely How I Let My Mind Float" that stands as one of De La Soul's best non-album tracks.

"En Focus," produced by Pos, intentionally uses the same sample source that Masta Ace used on his 1990 single "Music Man": "Nothing Is the Same" by Grand Funk Railroad. He told *GQ* he was imagining Masta Ace hearing it and being impressed ("Like, 'Yo, the way they flipped it was dope!'").

One of Prince Paul's contributions to *Buhloone* was making phone calls that led to getting James Brown's horn players the JB Horns—Maceo Parker, Fred Wesley, and Pee Wee Ellis—on the album. Wesley and Parker were also part of the Horny Horns; another P-Funk connection for De La Soul. Paul and Pos had been listening together to one of the albums Maceo Parker released in the early nineties (likely *Roots Revisited* or *Mo' Roots*) when they had the idea.

Mase told 247HH working with Parker, Wesley, and Ellis for two weeks was his most memorable studio moment; it made him feel closer to being an instrument-playing musician himself. The musicians picked the studio they worked in, the Magic Shop in the SoHo neighborhood of Manhattan, and they spent two weeks in the studio working through the music. They brought other musicians from Maceo Parker's band: his brother Melvin (the drummer on James Brown's "I Got You (I Feel Good)" and "Papa's Got a Brand New Bag"), guitarist Rodney Jones, organist Larry Goldings, and flutist Frank Wess (who was on dozens of albums with the Count Basie Orchestra in the fifties and sixties).

The presence of those seasoned musicians on the album connects it to a large history of musicianship as a business, evoking the complex history of big business taking advantage of creatives, especially African Americans, for financial gain. It's a topic De La Soul covers on *Buhloone Mindstate*, especially on the same song those musicians play on. "Patti Dooke" also features Guru from Gang Starr, voicing the chorus. The song integrates samples from the movie *The Five Heartbeats*, with characters talking about how the music industry pushes Black artists to change their sound to appease white audiences ("Crossover ain't nothing but a double cross"). The track is worded in enigmatic De La fashion, but also carries a direct message about not deviating from artistic impulses for commercial success.

The second verse, from Pos, hits clearest, with lines about not "comprising any of my styles to gain a smile," plus a part where he contrasts the label's interest ("the boys from Tommy plant bridge crossin' to a larger community") with their own community of like-minded artists. In the third verse, he directly calls out white label executives who plunder the cultural legacy and history of Black music for their own financial gain: "White boy Roy cannot feel it / but the first to try and steal it / dilute it, pollute it, kill it." The song includes the mantra about blowing up but not going pop, in defiance of record label intentions.

Buhloone Mindstate has these streaks of direct expression, but they're often cloaked in wording that at first seems to obfuscate. De La Soul always had their own language. On *Buhloone Mindstate* they seemed at first listen to have reached a new level of obtuse. In 2023, writer Sheldon Pearce called it "a concept album where the concept is a secret." Danyel Smith put it this way in her *Spin* review at the time of the album's release: "No matter the craftsmanship of the beats or the rhymestyles, the question must come up, what the fuck are they talking about?"

"I Am I Be" is one of the songs where the topic is made clear: identity. Who you are and how you live your life within the particular moment of history that you're born into, in the face of the commercial and sociocultural forces in motion around you. The track starts with Shortie's voice, "I am Shortie, I be four eleven," and throughout is a series of other similar statements from the likes of Chris Lighty, Bob Power, Dres, and more. But the heart of the song is the verses: one from Dave in between two from Posdnuos. Pos's own verses are frank, in-the-moment reflections on his life the likes that hip-hop hadn't seen at that point. Think about "introspective" rap songs up to 1993 and it'll either be a love song (LL Cool J at the piano, breathlessly saying, "I need love") or a tribute to someone who died (Ice Cube's "Dead Homiez," Pete Rock & CL Smooth's "They Reminisce Over You [T.R.O.Y.]").

On "I Am I Be," Pos reflects on his life story: his upbringing, his mom's passing, his daughter being born, his struggles to maintain a romantic relationship. At the outset of the song, and repeated as somewhat of a chorus, he picks up the album's record-industry theme: "I am Posdnuos, I be the new generation of slaves / here to make papes to buy a record exec rakes." He also describes internal struggles among the Native Tongues; mainly lack of communication ("some tongues who lied and said we'll be natives to the end / nowadays we don't even speak"). That piece ended up being one of the most quoted, something Pos later expressed regret over. He was rhyming based on how he felt that day, about his friends, and it was cemented on wax forever.

It's not the only reference on the album to Native Tongues being over. On "In the Woods," Pos casually drops, "Yo, that native shit is dead." On "Breakadawn" there's "I tell you, Jungle Brothers on the run," which is both a clever reference to a 1988 JBs song ("On the Run") and a sign the groups were growing apart.

(Intentional or not, "on the run" also feels like a true representation of the out-there-on-their-own situation the Jungle Brothers themselves were in, with their experimental LP *Crazy Wisdom Masters* rejected by Warner Bros. and eventually released in neutered form as 1993's *J Beez wit the Remedy*.)

Dave's verse is more abstract, harder to parse completely, though it has beautiful turns of phrase ("I choose to run from the rays of the burning sun / and dodge a needle washing up upon a sandy shore."). Posdnuos wrote Dave's verse for him. That's one of the less-publicized aspects of De La Soul's music: the extent to which they created the words and the music together, for each other and for the group overall.

Terms like "producer" and "DJ" don't properly reflect the way that all of them contributed to words, music, and song structure, from the beginning. Mase told *Serato Unscripted* in 2019 that De La Soul has "always been a collective thing and an individual thing."

The music for "I Am I Be" was built around something Prince Paul made on four-track cassette for his own purposes. It was music for chilling out at home that he never planned to have anyone rhyme on. It was built largely off the beginning of Lou Rawls's "You've Made Me So Very Happy," produced by David Axelrod. He added harmonica from a Snooky Pryor song, Eddie Harris saxophone, guitar from a Jimmy Ponder cover of "While My Guitar Gently Weeps," and more elements. When Posdnuos stopped by Prince Paul's house and heard it, he was immediately drawn to it. "The hairs on my skin stood up, I just loved it," he told Oliver Wang.

The music for "I Am I Be" appears earlier in the album, a sort of preface, on the track "I Be Blowin'," essentially a five-minute Maceo Parker riff on the tune. The title comes from how the song starts, with Parker saying, "I am Maceo, I be blowin' the soul out of this horn." It was an unusual choice to include a straight-ahead jazz track on a hip-hop album (even Guru's jazz-oriented *Jazzmatazz Vol. 1.*, released the same year, doesn't have any instrumental sections that long). This helps accentuate the feeling that "I Am I Be" represents the heart and soul of the album.

On Mike Pizzo's podcast *Let the Record Show*, Talib Kweli described "I Am I Be" as one of his favorite songs of all time, highlighting the poetry of the track and the autobiographical content of the verses: "These are things that I had never heard in a hip-hop record, all in one record." In a *Washington Post* fifty years of hip-hop playlist, author Jeff Chang described it as a song that made him realize he could grow old with hip-hop. "It's about generations, it's about community, it's about family. It's them telling their stories." The song was a clear precursor to the legions of more autobiographical and introspective hip-hop records that came in its wake.

Another *Buhloone* song that seems prescient in a different way is one that was thrown together: "Long Island Wildin'." The title comes from a clip of Tricky Tee saying, "Long Island is wildin'," but the bulk of the track consists of rap in Japanese from Takagi Kan and the trio Scha Dara Parr (SDP), whom De La Soul met when they toured Japan in the fall of 1989, after the release of *3 Feet High and Rising*. The Japanese artists were in New York while *Buhloone Mindstate* was being recorded. Prince Paul was working with them on a remix and invited them to the studio while De La Soul was recording. The Japanese rhymes include a quick verse about flying to NYC and being invited to the studio, getting there on time, and dropping the line they're about to drop, in English: "Yes, yes, y'all, we don't stop!"

On the album it's a quick interlude. The group vetoed Prince Paul's contrarian impulse to make it the first song on the album. It is prescient in the sense that it documents a glimpse of the growing international scope of hip-hop's influence, which has multiplied over the decades since.

Two other interludes are the closest to "bug-out" skits on the album: a clip of Prince Paul ("Paul's Revenge") complaining that *The Source* miscredited a Slick Rick track that Paul worked on, and a clip of Dave sped up to sound like he's orgasming ("Dave Has a Problem . . . Seriously"), making *Buhloone* one of three De La Soul albums with fake orgasm sounds.

"In the Woods" was produced by Mase. It's a track he created for KRS-One, but when it became clear that wasn't happening, he used it for De La. The song includes more rhymes from Shortie than the rest of the album; she has a proper verse on it, one that she wrote. There's also a Posdnuos line that's among the group's most repeated lyrics, what *The Source* used to call a "hip-hop quotable": "Fuck being hard / Posdnuos is complicated!" The song starts with what sound like jingle bells. That combined with the woods reference makes me want to propose this as a Christmas song. To add to that is an image of Dave as an elf, within something he related to Oliver Wang about the process of recording the song. He said he was high, and he heard two different voices in his head, like an alter ego he was conversing with. "I'm talking back and forth with this other voice; I'm an elf." Like he says in the song, "It's that funky shit that be beyond understanding."

"Ego Trippin' (Part Two)," the album's second single and video, was also Mase's brainchild, built around Al Hirt's "Harlem Hendoo." The song is a sequel of sorts to Ultramagnetic MCs' pioneering debut single "Ego Trippin'," from 1986, the song Prince Paul cited as influential to his sampling approach. In De La Soul's version, the MCs humorously indulge their egos ("I'm the greatest MC in the world!") while also paying tribute to dozens of hip-hop classics. Tunes referenced include "La Di Da Di," "Sucker MCs," "T.R.O.Y.," "White Lines" by Grandmaster Flash and the Furious Five, Boogie Down Productions' "I'm Still #1" and "The Bridge Is Over," Big Daddy Kane's "Ain't No Half-Steppin'," and many more.

With some of those songs, the parts they use include references to other music of the past (Billy Joel's "It's Still

Rock and Roll to Me," for one), adding layers to the hip-hop onion they're peeling back. They also reference their own singles—"Potholes" and "Ring Ring Ring," at the least. The song has one of the best nods toward suburbia in their catalog, from Dave: "I've got the trees in my backyard / and it's hard for them to tell lies to me." The unspoken context is the lies circling within the music business, and Dave's impulse to retreat from the industry.

The video, directed by Frank Carpenter, took the sarcastic side of the song and capitalized on it, creating a parody of extravagance in hip-hop. They're mainly poking fun at De La themselves, as unlikely to bask in fame and luxury the way other artists do. It caused an unlikely beef of sorts. 2Pac took the clip as an intentional parody of his "I Get Around" video. The group didn't intend it that way, though the director may have been aware of the connection. Posdnuos has expressed in various interviews the regret that he wasn't able to clarify their intentions with 2Pac before he was killed in September 1996, at age twenty-five.

Posdnuos has said the *Buhloone Mindstate* album was unsatisfying to him, like something was missing. In contrast, Mase has cited it as his favorite. Among De La Soul fans, the LP has grown in stature over time, which the group has attributed to listeners aging and maturing. Chris Rock has said it's one of his all-time favorite records. It's why he asked Prince Paul to produce his 1997 album *Roll with the New*, which won a Grammy for Best Comedy Album.

In the *NPR* retrospective piece on the album, Dante Ross pointed to *Buhloone* as the album that set De La Soul outside of hip-hop, "almost like an alternative rock band." Between the marketing of *3 Feet High and Rising* and the extensive, diverse touring that the group did, including internationally, De La Soul already had an audience that varied in age, race, background, and genre interests. It was an era when the alternative rock "industry" looked to hip-hop acts to indicate diversity and hipness, a sense that they were with the times. Ice-T and Ice Cube both played the Lollapalooza festival (as Tribe would, in '94). This is all after the Run-D.M.C./Aerosmith "Walk This Way" hit, the Public Enemy/Anthrax version of "Bring the Noise," and the success of the Beastie Boys in playing to both rock and hip-hop audiences. There was a continual buzz in music media around potential rap/rock crossovers. The 1993 soundtrack to the movie *Judgment Night* was built around the real or hoped-for intersections among hip-hop and alternative rock. In an oral history of the soundtrack album, for *Rolling Stone*, Christopher Weingarten described the makeup of the album as "a who's who of *Alternative Nation*, *Headbangers Ball*, and *Yo! MTV Raps*—a record label exec making the most of three youth-culture undergrounds."

For their part of the *Judgment Night* soundtrack, a song called "Fallin'," De La Soul was paired with Scottish indie band Teenage Fanclub, whose album *Bandwagonesque* had been *Spin*'s album of the year in 1991 (chosen over *Nevermind*, famously). Posdnuos told Jeff Weiss for *L.A. Weekly* that they picked Teenage Fanclub precisely because they hadn't heard of them before. De La Soul traveled to a studio in Cheadle Hulme, England, outside Manchester, without knowing anything about Teenage Fanclub or their music. In the *Rolling Stone* oral history, Raymond McGinley of Teenage Fanclub says they felt like they "won the gold medal" in terms of which group they were paired with, because they were De La Soul fans.

While they sat together in the lobby of the studio, trying

to figure out how to approach the song, Tom Petty's "Free Fallin'" video came on the TV. De La Soul got the idea of sampling it, and making the song be from the perspective of a rapper falling off after success. They sent someone to the closest CD store to find the Tom Petty record, so they could build off it. They used a snippet of Petty's voice, not the music, plus the bass line from "Fly Like an Eagle" by the Steve Miller Band, which they recalled Biz Markie using on "Nobody Beats the Biz." Teenage Fanclub played the music and sang backing vocals. The song ends with Maseo goofin' (mimicking Duice's "Dazzey Duks") and laughing—foreshadowing their next bout with alternative-rock success.

By the end of 1993, Prince Paul's group Gravediggaz had signed a deal with Gee Street, the UK label that released some of the "alternative" hip-hop (PM Dawn, New Kingdom) that had come in the wake of De La Soul. The album, called *Niggamortis* in the UK and *6 Feet Deep* for the US release, came out in the summer of '94 and was seen as introducing a new subgenre of rap: horrorcore. By then, RZA's group Wu-Tang Clan had blown up, representing a new era for the idea of what a hip-hop group could be.

8. WHAT'S GOING ON: THE TURNING POINT THAT WAS *STAKES IS HIGH*

When Prince Paul first started working with De La Soul, he thought of it as temporary. He'd help them get started, teach them how to make a record, and move on to something else. To his surprise they asked him back for a second album, and then a third. They considered him part of the group. Often described by critics and reporters as a producer, De La Soul saw him as a friend and mentor, not to mention an equal member of the group, during the first part of their career: Plug 4.

Early during the recording sessions for De La Soul's fourth album, Prince Paul quit. It was "over petty stuff," he told Open Mike Eagle on *What Had Happened Was*. An argument with Posdnuos over a sample of a hi-hat was reportedly the last straw, but it was more about differing perspectives on the music itself. Prince Paul's playful, humor-driven approach was in contrast, or conflict even, with De La Soul's frame of mind at that point in time. In 2016 Posdnuos told interviewer Eddie "Stats" Houghton that Prince Paul was bringing to the table ideas that were "just a little too zany, still a little too funny" for where the rest of the group was at. Mase agreed, telling *Serato*

Unscripted, "Things weren't really funny and fun during that time period."

Buhloone Mindstate sold two hundred thousand copies initially, per the *New York Times*, which was significantly less than the first two albums. That comparative decline in commercial success led to what Mase described to *GQ* as "blackballing," a lack of support for the group by their label and within the industry.

After the release of *Buhloone Mindstate*, De La Soul toured with A Tribe Called Quest across the United States. The group have recounted in various interviews that a career turning point came during that tour, when Lyor Cohen took them aside to tell them they'd need to "tighten their belts" financially. Meanwhile, Tribe released their third album, *Midnight Mauraders*, in November 1993 (the title referred in part to the late-night recording sessions of the Native Tongues groups). Tribe had followed up one instant classic (1991's *The Low End Theory*) with another, and seemed to be hotter than ever. De La Soul, by contrast, didn't know whether they were rising or falling.

For De La Soul, the making of their fourth album was a pivotal point in their career—"a point of reckoning," as Jolicoeur phrased it to *HipHopDX* in 2016. The business side of making music was wearing them down. Their third album was now considered a commercial failure, by the label and to some extent by the group. It was an era in hip-hop when the East Coast–West Coast beef was the big media story, with the Notorious B.I.G. and 2Pac as megastars and Bad Boy Records emerging as a presence. De La Soul began to wonder if there was still a place in music for them.

Stakes Is High was the first album where they started the creative process with a message they wanted to convey, and a title to reflect it. The phrase they chose to reflect their state of mind came from conversations with Dave's cousin Fudge. They considered him a hip-hop philosopher, and while philosophizing about the hip-hop industry and where De La Soul fit in, he told them, "Stakes is high for De La right now." The resulting album at times carried a serious, almost apocalyptic message, about the state of hip-hop, the industry, and of the country itself.

The group felt the weight of comparison to what else was going on in hip-hop at the time. They needed to "do something that could at least hang" with other artists of the era, as Dave phrased it to *HipHopDX*. They felt they needed to come out with a statement album that would make an impression and differentiate them from whatever the public perception was of De La Soul.

Dave was the driving force behind the music on *Stakes Is High*, the main producer for the album. Mase told *HipHopDX* it was the moment when Dave "came into his own as a full-fledged producer" within the group, compared to earlier albums when Posdnuos, Prince Paul, and Mase drove more of the production. It was also the first LP where they used outside producers, albeit fewer than they would going forward. Of the seventeen tracks on *Stakes Is High*, two were produced solely by others (Spearhead X on "Dinninit" and Skeff Anselm on "Big Brother Beat") and two were co-produced with others (O.Gee of D.I.T.C. on "4 More" and Jay Dee a.k.a. J Dilla on "Stakes Is High").

The sound of the album strips away what might be considered the artsy qualities of *Buhloone Mindstate*, without going back toward anything resembling the layered, eclectic approach of the first two albums. Instead, it's a clean, crisp, relatively minimalist sound with a fair amount of R&B

influence (even as they continued to mock R&B). "Baby Baby Baby Baby Ooh Baby" takes that mocking the furthest. It parodies R&B-driven rap songs, but is also a good version of the same. Maseo reprises a WRMS DJ bit for the song's ending.

The album introduction is a series of voices talking about the first time they heard Boogie Down Productions' 1987 debut album *Criminal Minded*, an influential album for the group and for hip-hop. Those clips were recorded on Posdnuos's answering machine. He changed his message so when someone called, they'd hear him asking them to leave a message describing when they first heard *Criminal Minded*. The responses are a quick audio tour of early hip-hop culture: parties, rap battles, NYC locations. This serves to root the album in hip-hop history before the group tries to carve out their own statement of intent. It's also a grounding in where De La Soul came from, as hip-hop fans first.

The musical track these clips appear over was originally an unused remix to the *Buhloone Mindstate* song "Eye Patch." This is why Pos's lyrics to the two songs are similar ("Channeling in sing so my what brings"). He right away establishes the grim perspective within which De La is reestablishing their greatness: "De La Soul is here to stay, like racism!"

The intro set the "stakes" of the title as not just De La Soul's career but hip-hop itself. In 2003 Dave told *Uncut* that what they were witnessing in hip-hop made them feel like *Stakes Is High* was an album they *had* to create: "Hip-hop is dear to us, and we felt it was being destroyed." Pos has called the album their version of Marvin Gaye's *What's Going On*, an act of digesting what they saw happening around them.

The first track after the intro, "Supa Emcees," is a lament that asks, "Whatever happened to the MC?" Dave references Pinocchio's Theory, the P-Funk concept that if you fake the funk, your nose will grow (see the 1977 single by Bootsy's Rubber Band). That's their MO on *Stakes Is High*, to call out those "faking the funk." The rhymes throughout the album are direct. The group's not speaking in code, they're not clouding their intentions through poetry. There are some party songs, but the moments of humor are minor, not funny for funny's sake.

Their beefs are with so-called gangsta rappers aligning themselves with Mafia figures who don't align with Black culture, with "playas" emphasizing their money and luxury goods over their craft ("champagne-sipping money fakers," Dave calls them on "The Bizness"). In "Dog Eat Dog" they threaten to leave music entirely if hip-hop can't figure out something new to say. "Brakes" calls back to Kurtis Blow ("The Breaks," 1980) while reminiscing about their own rise to rap stardom and the challenges that come with trying to stay humble and grounded in an industry where everyone wants something from you.

This is their first album to have a title track; "Stakes Is High" the song is a concentrated expression of their concern for hip-hop and the world, with co-production by Jay Dee, a.k.a. J Dilla, of the group Slum Village. Now broadly acknowledged as one of the most innovative producers in hip-hop history, James Dewitt Yancey had his own unique approach to time and rhythm. What he created for "Stakes Is High" uses a short piece from Ahmad Jamal's "Swahililand" (off *Jamal Plays Jamal*, 1974), over drums he programmed, to set a serious mood filled with emotional nuance. In a sample of 1973's "Mind Power," James Brown's voice intones "vibe, vibrations," an enigmatic refrain that adds to the mood.

The music sets the scene for some of Pos's and Dave's bluntest rhymes, focusing on everything around them that is deteriorating, from rappers trying to live out their violent dreams to the effects of drugs and materialism on the Black community. "A meteor has more right than my people," Pos declares, with bittersweet wordplay.

The song begins with a clip of a homeless man speaking. This is someone who was outside Platinum Island Studios while they worked on the album; Maseo would stop and chat with him. They recorded him talking about his life and then had him say the lines about "stakes is high," trying to broaden their message of urgency beyond just their group or even hip-hop. They wanted to demonstrate the universality of the phrase, that stakes is high for everyone.

In the song, Posdnuos also proclaimed, "Native Tongues has officially been reinstated!" It was a joyous moment for fans, but it was less a literal statement than a feeling, part of the album's pronouncement that De La Soul's style of hip-hop was here to stay.

On the twenty-seventh anniversary of the album's release, Pos shared on Instagram a short clip of the demo version of the song, before Dilla's contribution. The demo used a sample of the Heath Brothers' "Smilin' Billy Suite Pt. II," which Q-Tip sampled in his production for Nas's *Illmatic* song "One Love."

In an alternate reality the "Stakes Is High" J Dilla track might not have been used by De La Soul at all. Pos was over at Q-Tip's house in New Jersey, and they were listening to various Jay Dee beats that he had sent as potential Tribe Called Quest material. One of the tracks was what became "Stakes Is High." Posdnuos was so wowed by it that he acted completely disinterested, out of fear that the track would be used by Tip if he drew attention to it. After he left, he reached out to Jay Dee directly to ask for the beat. Pos told *World Café* that the Dilla beat elevated the song and the album. It "felt like God, it felt biblical"—capturing the cinematic, monumental sense of urgency that they intended with the phrase and theme "stakes is high."

Despite all the serious messages, *Stakes Is High* is a party album too. For all the group's complaints about R&B—on past albums and on this one—there are songs like "4 More," with the vocal duo Zhané singing the hook sweetly over minimalist production geared toward instant impact. Other key collaborators on the LP include Common on "The Bizness" and Mos Def on "Big Brother Beat." Mos Def (now known as Yasiin Bey) was close friends with one of De La Soul's dancers, and Mase also met him while DJing a poetry reading hosted by Mos and his mother. Mos Def started hanging out with De La, and was present in the studio throughout the recording of *Stakes Is High*. He and his collaborators Medina Green—the group of DCQ, Magnetic, Lord Ato and Jah-Born—were among those playing the dice game heard at the beginning of "Stakes Is High." Posdnuos has given Mos Def credit for inspiring him to step up his rhyming game on the album, to focus more on his flow.

Mos Def's feature on "Big Brother Beat" was his first high-profile appearance on an album, followed a few months later by a couple of songs on Da Bush Babees' album *Gravity* (including "The Love Song," produced by Posdnuos). This was a year before Mos Def's first single "Universal Magnetic," and two years before the album *Mos Def and Talib Kweli Are Black Star*.

DE LA SOUL

The Chicago rapper Common was more established, with two albums (as Common Sense), and a well-regarded single about the state of hip-hop ("I Used to Love H.E.R."). "The Bizness" broadened the attention given to his rhyming skills, among hip-hop fans, foreshadowing his subsequent rise as a star.

Pos and Dave each had solo songs on the album. Pos's was "Wonce Again Long Island," a head-knocker establishing his commitment to hip-hop even in tough times. Dave's was "Itzsoweezee (Hot)," built off a track Posdnuos produced. It started as an attempted remix for the Naughty by Nature song "Feel Me Flow," in response to a Tommy Boy request. Pos had abandoned it because he didn't feel like it would do anything to take the original song further. He let Dave hear it; he liked it and wanted to rhyme on it. It was the last song recorded for the album.

Stakes Is High was a confidence boost for the group, showing they could produce on their own and reestablish their place within hip-hop. It kept De La Soul going as an entity and set them up for the next phase of their career. Mase told *Okayplayer* that sales-wise the album was "as successful as it needed to be . . . [it] let us know there's a place in this music industry for us." It provided a positive answer to an existential question; as Mase phrased it to *HipHopDX*, "Are we still going to exist here?"

The album's title track has its own place in hip-hop history. After J Dilla passed away in 2006, "Stakes Is High" was used to demonstrate the versatility of his skill. Posdnuos and Talib Kweli even performed the track as part of a 2009 memorial concert in Los Angeles where an orchestra, put together by Miguel Atwood-Ferguson, performed Dilla's music. It can be heard on the 2022 album *Timeless: Suite for*

Ma Dukes. In that version, the words "love" and "vibrations" become a mantra for the crowd to chant together, echoing off and counterbalancing the idea of stakes being high—while the memorial angle makes clear the ultimate stakes are life and death.

Another track from *Stakes Is High* was performed at the White House in 2016, at the final musical event of the Obama administration (the televised version was titled *BET Presents: Love & Happiness*). The group was invited by Barack and Michelle Obama, and one of the songs that Michelle requested was "The Bizness." In 2023 Pos told *Drink Champs* how hard it was to perform "The Bizness" when he looked over and saw the First Lady singing along to every word. For De La Soul, performing at the White House was a huge achievement, and a memorable party. While presenting Questlove's recap, *Okayplayer* dubbed it, "The blackest night in White House history."

9. THAT NEW-MILLENNIUM FEEL: THE *ART OFFICIAL INTELLIGENCE* "TRILOGY"

Stakes Is High achieved what De La Soul wanted. It cemented the group's status as hip-hop veterans that would continue to make creative music, in touch with their past successes yet much different from them. Prince Paul has said it's his favorite De La Soul album, despite his lack of involvement. Meanwhile, he was continuing to carve out his own idiosyncratic lane within hip-hop. In 1996 he released a deeply strange, dark album of musical psychotherapy called *Psychoanalysis: What Is It?* on WordSound Recordings. To his surprise, Tommy Boy asked to reissue it, a year later, to give it a broader release. The description on the back cover reads, "This album is a compilation of senseless skitstyle material that was slapped together by Prince Paul for his own ill enjoyment." In 1999, he released a unique pet project, *A Prince among Thieves*, that resembled an aural cinematic street-opera in rap form (a true precursor of *Hamilton*). The main character was played by rapper Breeze Brewin, of Juggaknots, with a whole host of rappers as guests. Pos and Dave are cast, against type, as crack addicts.

For the five years in between *Stakes Is High* (1996) and their next album, De La Soul focused on playing live and taking care of their families. In 1997 they toured with 311 in the US and played festivals in Europe, plus the Tibetan Freedom Concert. In '98 they did some shows on the Lyricist Lounge tour with a pre-*Slim Shady LP* Eminem. In the summer of 2000 there was the Spitkicker tour focused on hip-hop lyricists (Common, Pharoahe Monch, Talib Kweli), while that fall brought the college Campus Invasion tour (with Wyclef and Black Eyed Peas).

Their concept for the next album was to make a three-disc epic where they could explore a variety of styles and ideas. It started as a joke, and then became a challenge to themselves. This was the era of the seventy-plus-minute hip-hop CD. Wu-Tang Clan had just released a double CD (*Wu-Tang Forever*). De La Soul's thinking at the time was "Let's top all of that and do a triple," Dave relayed to *Drink Champs*. Tommy Boy head honcho Tom Silverman suggested it made more business sense to release each album separately. Each record would get its own budget and its own promotion. Instead of one album cycle, they could set themselves up for a steady stream of attention over the course of a year if they spaced the three out by a few months.

Art Official Intelligence was the name, suggesting a futuristic vibe ("That new-millennium feel," Dave told *Billboard*) but also an opportunity to showcase their businesslike approach to creating art. It's art, and intelligent, but official business.

The first volume was *Art Official Intelligence: Mosaic Thump*, released in August 2000. The album cover shows the trio looking skeletal, like an anatomy diagram or a natural history display. After what they considered a "message album," the focus this time was on skill, on connecting with the original spirit of hip-hop—party music—while showcasing their ability to execute in multiple modes and styles. Dave told *The Fader* the LP was a chance "to wild out, bug out, have fun."

"Mosaic" in the title represents diversity, and the number of guests across the album. The "Thump" is the foundational beat of hip-hop—"Bangin' on the table like back in the days," as Dave put it to Pizzo of HipHopSite.com. Musically *Mosaic Thump* resembled a party. It built off the more contemporary sound of *Stakes Is High*, but was looser, with their sense of humor a key through line. The party vibe extended to the number of featured guests. De La Soul viewed *Mosaic Thump* as an opportunity to work with musicians they respected or always wanted to collaborate with. They increased the number of outside producers: Jay Dee, Rockwilder, Mr. Khaliyl (of Da Bush Babees), Supa Dave West, Ad Lib, Deaf 2 U, and even Prince Paul.

Supa Dave West produced "U Can Do (Life)" and "Copa (Cabanga)," and would go on to take a more prominent role in subsequent De La albums. He had been part of the group Hot Sauce, signed to Museum Music, an imprint of Elektra that Q-Tip started (other artists signed included Vinia Mojica and Consequence). Dave Jolicoeur and his cousin Fudge were visiting Phife in Atlanta, and Phife was listening to some of Supa Dave West's music, including what became "Copa (Cabanga)." He called Pos right away to tell him about the tracks, which he at first mistook for new J Dilla. Supa Dave West told TheRealHip-Hop.com he connected to De La because "we're like-minded . . . we have a lot of similar conversations musically."

Each of the singles had a guest artist: Redman on "Oooh," D.V. Alias Khrist on "Thru Ya City," and Chaka Khan on "All Good?" Five other songs on the album featured guests: the Alkaholiks, Xzibit, Busta Rhymes, Mike D and Ad-Rock of the Beastie Boys, Freddie Foxxx, and Busy Bee Starski. There was also an unreleased version of "Oooh" that featured Kurupt, and "All Good?" was originally going to feature Outkast.

De La Soul albums had been riddled with the voices of friends who happened to be in the studio while they were recording. The featured guests this time were chosen more purposefully. They were selected the way a sample or an instrument would be, in the spirit of "You know what would sound great here?" De La Soul described it to Pizzo as a matter of doing what felt right, and having fun trying to make a De La Soul song that also felt natural to the particular guest. Dave related the example of "Squat!," which featured two Beastie Boys: it "was just a vibe that Pos had like, 'Yo, I feel them on this track.'"

Posdnuos and Dave even wrote some of their guests' rhymes, in the case of Redman, the Beastie Boys, and possibly others. It was a way to test their own abilities, to see if they could write something that would resemble rhymes the guest would typically say, but which also fit into De La Soul's aesthetic. On "My Writes," Pos and Dave match the style and intensity of the hard-rhyming guests: Tash, J-Ro, and Xzibit. It's similar on the Busta Rhymes–featuring "I.C. Y'All," produced by Rockwilder with a mechanical groove that would fit on any Busta album.

This album's interludes, modernized bug-out pieces, play with the desire to put themselves in another artist's shoes, while also taking a playful jab at the practice of ghostwriting, a hot topic following some high-profile claims of famous artists using ghostwriters. There are three "ghost weed" skits on the album, fake advertisements for weed that makes you sound like another rapper—featuring Pharoahe Monch, Phife, and Black Thought. The label pressured them to find a big-name guest that would help sell the record. Attempts to get Mary J. Blige or Kelly Price didn't work out. They also considered Missy Elliott for "All Good?" It was their manager Corey Smyth who suggested he could get Chaka Khan. "All Good?" featuring Chaka Khan was the biggest US hit single for De La Soul in years, breaking into the Hot 100 for the first time since "Breakadawn" and into the Top 10 of the *Billboard* Rap chart for the first time since "Ring Ring, Ring." Note the question mark in the title of "All Good?" It's a happy-*sounding* song, a radio-friendly jam, but the group is still feeling the stress of people who want to take advantage of them. "It ain't all good, and that's the truth" is what Chaka Khan is singing as Dave scorns an ex-lover ("Tried to bring that fairy-tale life, you wanted horror") and Pos is keeping an eye out for schemers and fiends.

Even with the party vibe, and the overall focus on courting women out at the club, the album has its share of pain. The song "The Art of Getting Jumped" tries to put an entertaining spin on a real-life scary incident that Mase experienced while the group was on tour in Europe in 1996 or 1997. The verses narrate a similar story, to a disco beat. On the outro of the track, Mase tells the story ("This is dedicated to those punk motherfuckas out in Germany . . ."), one he elaborated on in a video interview with 247HH titled "Racist Turkish Gang Beat Me Up & Tried to Kill Me." In Frankfurt, Germany, he got jumped on his way into a club, was "beaten to a pulp" and had a gun put in his face. He ended up escaping and hiding out under a bridge. He described it as the scariest moment of his life.

The song is followed by Mase's first solo song on a De

La album, "U Don't Wanna B.D.S." It's about toughness—decrying rappers who pretend to be thugs but aren't prepared to live up to it. In the album press kit, Mase said it was inspired by someone he knew who was "going down a wrong path." The title spells out fully as "You don't wanna bust dat shit." It ends with a guest bit from one of the toughest voices in hip-hop, Long Islander Freddie Foxxx (a.k.a. Bumpy Knuckles), that's more like a speech than a rhyme, accentuating Mase's point. Foxxx's presence ties the album back to their Long Island beginnings, similar to how Busy Bee's guest track ("Words from the Chief Rocker") is a reminder that De La Soul's music, and the party vibes of *Mosaic Thump*, are rooted in the earliest days of hip-hop music and culture.

What *Vibe* considered De La Soul's "most contemporary offering yet" was described as "their most formulaic album to date" in the *Village Voice*. The pursuit of a De La Soul feeling within a listener-friendly, disco-party sound felt to some critics like an outright bid for commercial success—as if De La Soul weren't always interested in selling more albums.

Originally the second *AOI* album was planned for March 2001, and the third for June. Instead, it was December before *AOI: Bionix* was released. It followed a similar pattern to the first, with a contemporary sound and thoughtfully chosen guests—though fewer, and more often tasteful singers (Glenn Lewis, Yummy Bingham) than hard-edged rappers. The guest emcees are decidedly laid-back: B-Real, Devin the Dude, and Slick Rick. The guest on "The Sauce," Philly Black, was the kid Jeff from the early days, now an adult and a rapper of his own.

Compared to the first *AOI* album, on *Bionix* they dialed

down the party atmosphere, dialed up the use of Supa Dave West as producer (six tracks this time), and experimented more.

"Simply," produced by Supa Dave West, turns the synths from Paul McCartney's "Wonderful Christmastime" into a funky stroll (Does that make it a down-low Christmas song as well?). On the first verse, Dave mimics the rhyming cadence of Greg Nice from Nice & Smooth. On the podcast *People's Party with Talib Kweli*, Posdnuos relayed that Dave wanted him to rhyme as Smooth B, but he refused. So Dave did his own Smooth B impersonation later in the track. The song segues into an interlude ("Simply Havin'") that serves as an outro and another tribute to their friends in A Tribe Called Quest, with Pos mimicking the flow of Tribe's "Footprints," with a sample from it at the end (Q-Tip: "The rap is in control").

The lone single, "Baby Phat," featuring Yummy Bingham and Devin the Dude, was also produced by Supa Dave West. The emcees mimic the punchy feeling of the music in the cadence of their rhymes, while telling women not to worry about fitting the "perfect" beauty standard (Dave: "You ain't in this alone / I got a tummy too"). Across the album, rhymes are focused on attracting women: seeking love relationships on a few tracks, and purely sex on both the Slick Rick–featuring "What We Do (For Love)" and the surreal porn scenario "Pawn Star," featuring Shell Council (an enigmatic figure; internet searches come up empty). On the more relationship-oriented "Special," Dave takes an all-business approach that echoes the group's later-career focus on putting in work: "What I'm proposin' is a joint account . . . let's take our lil business and incorporate it."

On "Trying People," one of the group's most introspective

songs, Dave spells out what the other women-focused songs dance around: "I want a wife." Written and recorded soon after the 9/11 terrorist attacks, he had mortality on his mind. There's a line that would be quoted often after Jolicoeur's passing: "When I'm gone / make sure the headstone reads, 'He did it for us.'" Produced by Deaf 2 U, the duo of Pos's brother Lucious "Luck" Mercer and Neal "Purp" Forrester, the song has been mentioned by De La Soul as one of their all-time favorites. Pos's verse is just as frank as Dave's about relationship troubles, the battle between career and making time for family. The overall message is "we're trying."

The somber "Held Down" takes the perennial De La Soul theme of individuality in a serious direction, with life and death as the stakes. Posdnuos produced the song and delivers all the verses, with CeeLo Green singing the chorus. What in the first two verses seems like yet another list of De La grievances (backstabbers, beat biters, onetime friends feeling entitled to a piece of the group's success) turns inward in the second verse, with Pos realizing the only one left to point a finger at is himself: "The biggest suppressor could be your own ego lookin' for an excuse."

And then there's a stunning scene that Pos has said he based on real life. It takes the individuality versus following theme in a more apocalyptic direction. He's watching TV, and they're showing the aftermath of a Jonestown massacre–type scene, a cult leader taking followers to tragedy. His daughter asks, "Why are all the people sleeping on the floor?" His answer: "They were looking for God, but found religion instead." The skits that poke fun at a preacher named Reverend Do Good (voiced by studio engineer Troy Hightower) take on a different feeling after hearing that verse. In his review of *Bionix*, *Village Voice* critic Robert

Christgau declared, "Anyone who ever wondered what hip-hop might sound like when it grew up now has an answer."

Stakes Is High and the two *AOI* albums gave the group a new identity as seasoned veterans walking a line between commercial and artistic interests. At the same time, Prince Paul was continuing his path, with new personal and collaborative endeavors reflecting his sense of humor and anything-goes mentality. He sometimes seemed to be building a career that was purposely anti-careerist, yet finding success. His project with Dan "the Automator" Nakamura, Handsome Boy Modeling School, was titled after a scenario in the absurdist Chris Elliott sitcom *Get a Life*. Their approach to making music together was to play beats and ask each other, "Does this sound handsome to you?" Yet their 1999 album *So . . . How's Your Girl?* yielded rave reviews from critics and broke into the *Billboard* 200 albums chart.

10. LEGACY LIVES ON: INDUSTRY TURMOIL, *GRIND DATE*, AND GORILLAZ

The *AOI* trilogy was at one early point going to be broken out by member, with each album creatively driven by one of the three. The portion of that idea which remained was the plan to have the third installment be DJ-focused, put together by Maseo. On the title track for *Bionix*, Maseo called out, "Oh remember, *AOI* Part Three comin' soon! On some DJ shit . . ." But the DJ-focused third installment never happened. It looked like the planned 2001 release had turned into 2002, given the December '01 release of *Bionix*. Instead, the following year involved more tours, including a summer alt-rock festival called Unlimited Sunshine that featured Cake, the Flaming Lips, and Modest Mouse. The release of the third *AOI* would get wrapped up in recording industry turmoil.

The Warner Bros. Records–Tommy Boy partnership that started in 1985 ended in 2002. In the deal, the music catalog of Tommy Boy to that point in history became a part of Warner Music, while Tom Silverman retained the Tommy Boy trademark/name for his own future use as an independent label. (He'd soon after form a deal with Rhino Records to release new Tommy Boy material.) During the process of that sale, current Tommy Boy artists, including De La Soul, were free to find a new home. They were given the opportunity to shift to a different label within the WEA (Warner-Elektra-Atlantic) group of labels, or to find a new label on their own.

They considered Elektra Records, after being courted by Sylvia Rhone, who was an industry trailblazer (first woman, and first African American, to be CEO of a record label). When they realized Rhone had a very specific musical direction in mind, De La Soul turned down the offer. She wanted them to have one person, Timbaland, produce the whole LP. Timbaland was one of the hottest producers at the time, making his name over the previous decade working with Aaliyah, Missy Elliott, and many more. In 2003 alone he produced for Lil' Kim, Jay-Z, Alicia Keys, Zhané, and Nate Dogg, not to mention nearly entire albums for Missy Elliott and Bubba Sparxxx. Tying themselves to one producer, someone with as distinct a style as Timbaland, didn't appeal to De La Soul, who were accustomed to figuring out their own path for each album.

Instead of signing a deal, they worked on the album independently of a label, considering it the debut album release on their own AOI Records. But they partnered with an established label to distribute it. They signed with Sanctuary Urban Records Group, at that time a division of the London-based Sanctuary, which was the largest independent label in the United Kingdom. The year before, Sanctuary had purchased the Houston, Texas–based Music World Entertainment, founded and led by Mathew Knowles, father of Beyoncé Knowles. He was named the head of the Urban division of Sanctuary, and has said he was responsible for signing De La Soul.

The group set aside the idea of the third *AOI* in the process of signing the deal with Sanctuary. It seemed like an inappropriate first album to give a new record label. "It would have been wrong, we had to give them a straightforward De La Soul album," Posdnuos told *MVRemix*. That record, *The Grind Date*, released in October 2004, drew its inspiration from what their music career had become: a profession. The album art, designed by Morning Breath, Inc., was built off their actual calendar of scheduled work for 2005. The first track, "The Future," establishes De La Soul as an entity from the past and present, and the future—a creative force not going away anytime soon. Dave proclaims, "The name De La and the legacy built lives on!"

If the group considered the album "straightforward," that meant it reflected the beats-and-rhymes-forward approach of *Stakes Is High* and the *AOI* albums, but was even more no-frills. There are twelve songs in forty-nine minutes, with no skits, fewer sung hooks, fewer guests, and harder beats. "Just bring your beats / and bring your rhymes," they tell would-be competitors on the J Dilla–produced "Verbal Clap."

It's a skills-first album, in a hip-hop sense. Though De La Soul didn't want to be tied to one outside producer, they did end up working with other producers, including some of the hottest among fans of "pure" hip-hop in the era. *The Grind Date* was the first De La album where every song was credited to a producer outside the group. J Dilla produced two tracks (plus a bonus track for the international version), Jake One produced two, and Madlib produced two, with one song from 9th Wonder.

Supa Dave West returned to produce five of the twelve tracks, including the title track, which pulls a melody out of a twenty-one-minute prog-rock song by Yes ("Ritual

[Nous Sommes du Soleil]," off 1973's *Tales from Topographic Oceans*) and turns it into a boppy little loop that's almost bubblegum in tone, despite its origin. The optimistic music is both at odds and in alignment with the rhymes, about "putting in work."

The album was preceded a year earlier by a twelve-inch single the group independently released, on their own AOI label. It featured two of the Dilla-produced tracks: "Much More," featuring Yummy Bingham singing the chorus and DJ Premier doing an intro, and what ended up being a bonus track, "Shoomp," featuring Sean Paul. It incorporates the Tom Tom Club's "Genius of Love," chopped up Dilla-style, one of the more inventive uses of that song.

The official first single and video was for "Shopping Bags (She Got from You)," a hooky song produced by Madlib. It's almost a tired stand-up routine (POV: men who pay for their lovers' shopping sprees but don't get their expected benefit of sex in return) disguised as a radio anthem.

The other *Grind Date* single, "Rock Co.Kane Flow," featuring MF Doom, seems the epitome of the album's stated mission to push beats-and-rhymes-focused hip-hop toward the future while reinforcing De La Soul's legacy. The sample-free beat has a unique speed-up, then slow-down, then speed-up tempo. Producer Jake One told interviewer David Ma he was inspired by the programming on the Roc-A-Fella *Dynasty* album and wanted to play around more with pace. Jake One—now part of the duo Tuxedo with singer Mayer Hawthrone, and producer for a wide variety of hip-hop artists (Brother Ali, J. Cole, Rick Ross, Future, Chance the Rapper, etc.)—had previously done production for G-Unit and indie acts like Rasco, Encore, and Gift of Gab. He got connected to De La Soul through Jonathan

"Wordsayer" Moore, a Seattle hip-hop fixture. Jake One sent De La a CD of twenty or thirty different beats, and they picked out seven or eight. Two ended up on the album: "Rock Co.Kane Flow" and "Days of Our Lives," featuring Common.

There's a *Behind the Beat* video where Jake One shows how he built the beat for "Rock Co.Kane Flow" on the Ensoniq ASR-10. He demonstrates how he chopped up a vocal sample, drum sound, and keyboard part. The track almost seems to be taunting De La Soul to figure out a way to rap over it. It was another instance where Pos could hear in his head what artist would fit naturally over the music. He told *MVRemix* that the beat "literally almost called out the fact that Doom could be on it."

De La Soul knew Doom in some capacity all the way back to when he was known as Zev Love X, part of the group KMD. By the time of *The Grind Date*, MF Doom was one of the hottest hip-hop cult heroes: a metal mask-wearing MC who had created his own universe of productions and strange comic book–influenced rap.

The song leaked out ahead of the album release and was an underground hit. De La Soul got to the beat first, but 50 Cent also had a copy of it from Jake One and had rapped over it while working on *The Massacre*, before knowing that it was now De La's. The 50 version also leaked (as "Put a Hole in Yo Back"). Jake One told Gino Sorcinelli, "I was in New York when the 50 version dropped and I was hearing it everywhere." De La Soul incorporated "Rock Co.Kane Flow" into their live set as a perennial crowd-pleaser. They often performed it as the last song of their set, all the way through to 2023.

Around the time De La Soul were finishing up *The Grind*

Date, they recorded a collaboration with the English group Gorillaz that would become one of the biggest commercial successes of their career. Damon Albarn of the rock band Blur started Gorillaz in 1998 as a collaboration with his roommate at the time, the artist Jamie Hewlett. They would watch MTV and feel like they could do it better, that musicians were taking themselves too seriously. The idea was to have a virtual band, with characters and stories that could be told in music and art.

Their first album, produced largely by Dan "the Automator" Nakamura, had the hit song "Clint Eastwood," featuring the rapper Del the Funky Homosapien. He was added to the track at the last minute, but the song's success may have set a template for Gorillaz to have one or two hip-hop features on each album. Within the Gorillaz universe, the Del character had the power to conjure up the spirit of past musicians, which was meant to represent the act of creating hip-hop itself, since it's music built off music of the past that carries within it the output of musicians from throughout time.

For the 2005 follow-up, *Demon Days*, Gorillaz worked with the producer Brian Burton, a.k.a. Danger Mouse. Burton was best known for his *Grey Album*, which put instrumentals from the Beatles' White Album under vocals from Jay-Z's *The Black Album*. Albarn wanted to do a song with a hip-hop act again; it was Danger Mouse who suggested De La Soul as a good fit. Albarn and Burton sent Pos a few songs to choose from, and he gravitated toward one called "Kids with Guns." De La Soul flew to England for the recording sessions, without having met Albarn, Hewlett, or Burton. They immediately hit it off, settling into a weed-and-whiskey-fueled session where they spent a lot of time just goofing off, trying to make each other laugh.

Pos and Dave both wrote verses for "Kids with Guns," and brought them along to the session. But while in the studio, Dave heard the music for "Feel Good, Inc." and decided he wanted to rhyme on that track as well. He wrote and recorded a rhyme for it. Pos was also going to be on it, but was busy trying to finish up the *Grind Date* track "Shopping Bags." The Gorillaz album ultimately included "Feel Good, Inc.," featuring Dave and Mase, but not Pos. "Kids with Guns" is on the album, but without any rap verses.

"Feel Good, Inc." was one of the earliest songs Albarn and Burton did together, and had a space left in it where they wanted a rap to go. The finished track has a rap verse from Dave and a chorus built around Maseo's laugh, the laugh listeners heard at the end of the Teenage Fanclub collaboration "Fallin'" and at various points across De La Soul's albums. While recording the song, Albarn whispered Dave's rhymes in Mase's ear so he knew the right times to laugh.

It was a big hit, reaching #2 in the UK and #14 in the US. The song was nominated for the Record of the Year Grammy award, up against Kanye West's "Gold Digger," Gwen Stefani's "Hollaback Girl," Green Day's "Boulevard of Broken Dreams," and Mariah Carey's "We Belong Together." Green Day won that Grammy, but Gorillaz won another: Best Pop Collaboration with Vocals. It's the one Grammy that De La Soul has. (They were previously nominated for Best Rap Performance for "Me Myself and I," and Best Rap Performance by a Duo or Group for "Oooh.")

The experience started an intermittent collaboration with Albarn and Gorillaz that has continued to the present.

DE LA SOUL

De La Soul appeared on the third Gorillaz album *Plastic Beach* ("Superfast Jellyfish," also featuring Gruff Rhys of the Welsh band Super Furry Animals), and Pos is on the fifth album *Humanz* ("Momentz"). The deluxe version of sixth album *Cracker Island* has the De La–featuring "Crocadillaz." De La Soul, or Pos solo, have been a part of at least some dates on every Gorillaz tour since they first collaborated.

Mase told 247HH being part of Gorillaz is like being part of a circus, the cast of a musical, or a "whole new family." "And all I do is laugh, a laugh I got ridiculed for as a kid." "Feel Good, Inc." and the partnership with Gorillaz brought De La Soul back toward rock fans and further solidified their stature as "alternative" within the hip-hop world—as cult figures, even during an era when the music on their own albums sounded more in sync with commercial tastes and interests.

11. STARS UNLEASHED: THE DIGITAL VOID AND THE *ANONYMOUS NOBODY*

In 2005, after *The Grind Date*, the De La Soul deal with Sanctuary was dissolved—possibly because the group wasn't happy with the level of support they received. "We could have did that on our own and made more money off it," Pos told *Hard Knock TV*. The deal ending might have been related to the business situation at the label. Sanctuary had revenue declines, leading to the label's dissolution and absorption into Universal Music Group in 2007. In 2015, Dave told the website *Above Average Hip-Hop* that the moment their contract with Sanctuary ended "was the most liberating thing ever" and it pushed them on a path toward not signing with another record label.

The next decade for De La Soul was defined by two themes. One was their continued success as a hip-hop institution, touring on multi-genre lineups in the wake of their "alternative rock" success with Gorillaz. In 2006 they self-released a mix of unreleased material called *The Impossible: Mission TV Series—Pt. 1*. They lined up a partnership with Nike that yielded both shoes (limited-edition De La Dunks in 2005) and a digital mixtape, part of a Nike series of music meant to accompany exercise

(2009's *Are You In?*). In 2012, Pos and Dave teamed up with a French DJ duo called Chokolate and Khalid for an album, for Duck Down Music, where they took on new rap personas: Jacob "Pop Life" Barrow (Pos) and Deen Whitter (Dave). Titled *Plug 1 & Plug 2 Present . . . First Serve*, the album put a satirical focus on friends becoming overnight successes within an unfriendly industry.

The other path in this decade involved ongoing struggles with the availability of their earlier music, due to both industry tumult and contractual challenges. With most of their catalog, De La Soul essentially missed out on the MP3 era, when music sales shifted toward downloads via iTunes and other digital outlets. 2003 was when the iTunes store was launched, in coordination with major record labels, as a response to the extreme popularity of "illegal" downloads via Napster and other tools. By 2008, iTunes was the biggest music retailer in the US.

The one album De La Soul released during this time, *The Grind Date*, was available digitally, along with some lesser works Tom Silverman arranged to release through Rhino in 2004 (*Live at Tramps, NYC, 1996* and the compilation *De La Mix Tape: Remixes, Rarities and Classics*). But all the albums originally released on Tommy Boy—*3 Feet High and Rising* through *Bionix*—were under the control of Warner, which didn't see releasing them digitally as a priority, possibly out of concern for the potential of uncleared samples given the high-profile Turtles lawsuit.

The year 2014 brought the twenty-fifth anniversary of *3 Feet High and Rising*. De La Soul played a sold-out anniversary show at Irving Plaza in NYC, and did a UK anniversary tour. Yet the album itself was unavailable to consumers in any official manner. Fed up with the absence of their music in the marketplace, in early 2014 De La Soul took the step of gifting their fans their complete digital discography in exchange for an email address. They picked Valentine's Day for the release, a symbolic love letter. For twenty-four hours all their music would be free, as downloadable MP3s. The actual release was somewhat problematic, as the demand exceeded the bandwidth, so accessing the music wasn't as smooth as listeners anticipated. The reason was the way they went about it: linking to already existing files on pirate MP3 websites in other countries. The links for most of the albums were from a Russian website that already hosted pirate copies of the MP3s. These sites weren't set up to handle the amount of traffic that would come from De La Soul's offer to give fans these unavailable albums for free.

Around the same time, De La Soul was quietly working toward their next album, but with a musical approach that would purposely sidestep the legal and contractual risks involved with sampling. They were recording a more conventional De La Soul album titled *You're Welcome*, but set that aside to pursue a different idea, a collaboration with a live band. All the way back to the *De La Soul Is Dead* era, the group had pondered the idea of doing an entire album with live musicians. The closest they came before now were the horn players on *Buhloone* and some live performances, including the 1991 *Yo! MTV Unplugged* episode that paired De La, Tribe, LL Cool J, and MC Lyte with the band Pop's Cool Love.

Sometime in 2012, De La Soul did some shows with the Rhythm Roots Allstars, a Los Angeles–based group of musicians that made its name partly through live collaborations with hip-hop artists: Ghostface Killah, Talib Kweli, and others. De La invited the band to come to the studio and jam, mess around and see what happens. They hit on the idea of working toward an album by recording hours of jams and then using it to sample from. By sampling their own music, they would avoid all the challenges that come along with using other people's records.

Across three years, in between tour dates, De La Soul sporadically traveled to Electro-Vox Studios in Los Angeles for sessions with the Rhythm Roots Allstars. The studio had older analog equipment. In the documentary *We're Still Here (now) . . . a documentary about nobody*, Dave says the studio "looks like a fucking blast from the past," with an amazing sound and feeling. Producer Supa Dave West was there too. Posdnuos told *Creative Loafing* in 2015 that Supa Dave West's role was as co-producer and liaison: "to speak the language that we needed to speak between the musicians and hip-hop producers." Supa Dave West told *The Real Hip-Hop* that him being a drummer also played a factor in his involvement. Originally, they were going to use drummer Phillip "Fish" Fisher from Fishbone. Supa Dave West took over as drummer, working with the other musicians, but also helping produce on the hip-hop end.

They recorded the sessions with the band in L.A., but to create the album they worked together in Atlanta—building tracks from the sampled music, recording vocals, putting it all together, working with Supa Dave West and engineer Morgan Garcia. Ninety percent of what's heard on the finished album came from the Electro-Vox sessions.

De La Soul always wanted it to be an independent release. They've said everything they do going forward needs to be independent, even if they partner with a major in some way. They talked to different labels and potential partners along the way, but ended up pursuing an idea that

Mase was pushing: Kickstarter. Filmmakers Spike Lee and Nelson George had each used it to fund independent films. Mase also observed Ed O.G. doing it, but then not having a marketing budget to promote the finished album. In De La Soul's case, they wanted to find the right partners for marketing and promotion.

They hired Brandon Hixon, experienced with music marketing for Columbia Records and elsewhere, to be their campaign manager. He told *Forbes* he was initially nervous about the idea because of other recent hip-hop Kickstarters that had failed, citing a Geto Boys reunion album and an Onyx/M.O.P. collaboration. The group and Hixon decided to treat it like any other marketing product, but with the funding goal as the product. Hixon told *Forbes*, "We set up the release date, we set up the preplanning, we set up press, we set up everything like we would set up an album, but it was for the campaign."

In March 2015, De La Soul launched a crowdfunding effort through Kickstarter to raise money for the recording of the album *And the Anonymous Nobody...* The title came from how Dave would donate anonymously to charities. He'd give his name as Anonymous Nobody. This time the phrase would represent the funders of the Kickstarter campaign, the throng of people who gave small amounts of money to fuel something intangible and uncertain.

The group was concerned it would feel to fans like they were begging for money. The pitch on the Kickstarter page phrased "the ask" in terms of their musical legacy and their need for independence: "It's been essential that we find ways to fund, record, and release new music."

Funders of the Kickstarter effort could receive over forty different rewards, including unique collectables (autographed lyric sheets, De La sneakers, a boom box from Dave's collection, the exact MPC Maseo used to create "U Don't Wanna B.D.S.") and personal experiences with the trio. For prices ranging from $1,500 to $5,000, you could dig for records with Maseo, have a dinner date with De La Soul at the Red Rooster restaurant in Harlem, go sneaker shopping with Pos, toy-shop with Dave, or have a private DJ set with Maseo. For even more you could appear on the album itself, in a skit, or get the actual platinum plaque for *3 Feet High and Rising*, directly off the wall of Dave's office.

The goal was set at $110,000. They reached it within nine hours, doubled it on the second day, and ending up raising $600,874 from 11,619 supporters who gave an average of $50 each. It was the second-biggest Kickstarter campaign by a musician; Amanda Palmer had raised over a million dollars in 2012. *Forbes* declared De La Soul's campaign the fourth biggest in history by April 13, two weeks after its launch.

The excess money allowed the group to have bigger ambitions with their guest artists and musicians. They brought in horns and strings and recruited stars like Snoop Dogg and Usher. They estimated they spent an additional $250,000–$300,000 of their own money on the album, in addition to the Kickstarter funds.

In 2004, Posdnuos told *MVRemix* about the group's approach to guests, how when working on a song De La Soul will hear somebody's voice the way they hear where an instrument or a sample should go: "These people are nothing but instruments in the eyes of De La Soul."

On *Anonymous Nobody* that approach reached its apex. The album featured a diverse array of guests that might not seem on paper to fit the public perception of De La Soul, on songs that tilted in sound toward those guests. 2 Chainz is on the Dave-produced "Whoodeeni," and even with its futuristic vibe the tune seems ready-made for him. Roc Marciano slides just as naturally onto "Property of Spitkicker.com." "Lord Intended" is a strip-club-set hard rock song, with Justin Hawkins of the Darkness singing a part they originally imagined Axl Rose singing. For "Greyhounds," a singer they were auditioning sounded a lot like Usher, so they decided to instead get the real deal, Usher himself. "Snoopies," with Beastie Boys collaborator Money Mark among the co-producers, sounded to De La Soul almost like something Talking Heads would do—so they asked David Byrne to sing on it, and he said yes. Getting Byrne was "an administrative challenge," Masco told *The Barbershop Show*, but it worked out.

"Here in After," featuring Damon Albarn, with its alternative rock vibe, gives Dave a chance to contemplate mortality, longevity ("we're still here now"), and life after death, all in an atypical sing-song voice. He mentions specific losses: his parents and his cousin Fudge, who was murdered in Atlanta while working as a cab driver. Albarn's vocals are a strange emulation of the afterlife; he sounds adrift.

The video for "Royalty Capes" started with a clip of Dave talking about his own struggles with congestive heart failure, which started around the time of *The Grind Date*. He shows the LifeVest he wears, including while onstage. It's a wearable defibrillator, designed to deliver a treatment shock if dangerous heart behavior is detected.

With royal-proclamation horn fanfare as the primary backdrop, the song projects a spirit of legacy, declaring De La Soul to be hip-hop royalty while also demanding their proper royalties—a continual theme for a group still struggling with record label hardships. A poem is voiced throughout the song by Gina Loring, a poet, professor, daughter of *Blacula* actor William Marshall, and contributor to a song on De La's Nike album ("Poetic Greed"). Her words frame De La Soul as walking in the footsteps of historic forbears, Black creatives throughout time and beyond. They're collectively depicted as eternal: "We are an army of stars unleashed / the sky takes notes when we speak."

And the Anonymous Nobody . . . is a hip-hop album, but it carries the spirit of something like the Gorillaz albums, where any genre is fair game. There are R&B tracks, songs with an electronic vibe, and funk grooves. "Nosed Up" has some classic P-Funk-style voices, even one similar to Sir Nose D'Voidoffunk, the funk-denier with the Pinocchio nose. "Drawn," featuring the Swedish indie band Little Dragon (whom De La Soul met through Gorillaz), has no De La vocals until the last minute of its five-and-a-half-minute running time. And it still allows space for some of Pos's most soul-searching lyrics, about the impact of touring on his relationships, the disconnect between the image fans have of him and his own behavior: "'Hip hop lords'? Maybe, but my ways need laundering."

A bonus track called "Unfold" that appeared on the version sent to Kickstarter supporters might be their most surprising genre turn: it's a country-rap story-song, complete with a cowboy narrator, horses, saloon, poker game, and a high-noon showdown with a character named Tumbleweed Baker (the name of an actual singing cowboy actor in the late 1930s). They tried to get Willie Nelson, but couldn't; perhaps that's what relegated the song to "bonus" status. Dave told *Complex*: "We wanted Willie Nelson on that really bad . . . we pursued him over and over again after we got the first, second, third, fourth, and fifth no. He was unavailable to do it."

The song reminds us Dave Jolicoeur grew up listening to his parents' country albums. As a cartoonish C&W narrative, it also has its own unique place within the long continuum of country-rap conversations—what Chris Molanphy, in his 2023 book *Old Town Road* called, "a decades-long history of cross-pollination between hip-hop and country . . . [that] was always equal parts comedy and comity."

"Unfold" also ends up being another De La Soul track about mustering the strength to overcome individual obstacles. The narrator breaks into song at the end, singing about how to handle times when "the troubles of the land / grab hold 'round the mountains / valleys seem to swallow you whole." Riding off until the pastures unfold in front of you is his answer. When life is pushing you in a direction you don't like, veer off in another one.

12. CREATIVITY DOES FLOURISH: REISSUES, TRAGEDY, AND THE FUTURE

While promoting *Anonymous Nobody*, De La Soul had the chance to tell interviewers about their struggles with getting their earliest albums back out in the marketplace. A *New York Times* headline in August 2016, right before the release of *Anonymous Nobody*, put it like this: "De La Soul's Legacy Is Trapped in Digital Limbo."

"We spent years and years trying to figure this out with Warner," Pos told *New York Times* reporter Finn Cohen. The article included the perspective of Deborah Mannis-Gardner, whom the group worked with to clear samples for *Anonymous*. Her take was that Warner was concerned about whether the samples were originally cleared. "It becomes difficult opening these cans of worms," she said. "Were things possibly cleared with a handshake?"

Another potential complicating factor was the terms of the original contract not accounting for future music formats. Would the original sample agreements, which mention only the formats available back then (CD, tape, vinyl) even apply when it comes to digital formats like downloads and streams? By this point the music industry had largely shifted from downloads to streaming services like Spotify, Apple Music, Amazon Music, and Tidal. The group needed to figure out how to get their albums into the current digital-music marketplace.

In 2019, for a moment it seemed like the group's music would become available. Tom Silverman had reacquired the Tommy Boy catalog from Warner Music. Tommy Boy announced that De La Soul's earliest albums would be reissued and appear on streaming services. De La Soul shared the announcement, but also let everyone know they weren't being given their fair share of the profits. Their Instagram post went like this: "Dear Fans . . . The music WILL be released digitally. After 30 long years of good music and paying their debt to Hip Hop, De La Soul unfortunately, will not taste the fruit of their labor. Your purchases will roughly go 90% Tommy Boy, 10% De La." The post also included the hashtag "#thephantom2milliondollardebt," referencing a Tommy Boy claim that the group still owed them $2 million from the original contract they signed.

De La Soul shared their side of the story on the radio show *Sway in the Morning* that February (posted online as "De La Soul Is Getting ROBBED by Tommy Boy Records Still on Their 30th Anniversary"). In the interview, geared toward celebrating the thirtieth anniversary of *3 Feet*, they detailed why they thought Tommy Boy's offer was unfair, and why they were asking fans to not listen to the Tommy Boy streams when they went up. De La Soul would get 10 percent of the revenue. They had no reassurance that Tommy Boy was accounting for potential uncleared samples and were worried their 10 percent would end up going to handle sample lawsuits.

They shared their appreciation for Tommy Boy giving them creative freedom, but also said they've never received more than "pennies" from album royalties. They also felt like Tom Silverman did not understand hip-hop culture. The group put it in the context of the music industry taking advantage of artists, especially Black artists, throughout history. "People are really shady in this game," Maseo said. On Instagram they posted, "We regret that you and fans have been placed in the middle of this mess. De La Soul cannot afford negligent hurried business. We are fighting for our livelihood."

Hip-hop artists quickly jumped to support De La Soul in their struggle. Questlove called for a Tommy Boy boycott, asking listeners to resist playing the new streaming versions. Jay-Z, an owner and founder of Tidal, announced that it would not be hosting the Tommy Boy De La Soul streams. Nas asked his fans to join in the boycott. Q-Tip spoke up in support.

The attention built over the course of a week, with De La and their supporters using social media to spread the word. De La shared on Instagram that Tommy Boy said they'd negotiate a better deal, but only if the group agreed to keep the details confidential. Their request to fans became "Don't press Play" when the Tommy Boy streams are up.

The day before the albums were scheduled to appear on streaming services, *Variety* reported that Tommy Boy would be delaying the release. Maseo expressed gratitude to *Billboard* that their story was "finally being told," and Pos added, "Our story is told, but it definitely ain't over."

In February 2021, an episode of the animated TV show *Teen Titans Go!* fictionalized their story. Fittingly titled "Don't Press Play," the episode had this plot, per the Internet Movie Database: "The Titans must help De La Soul save their music after it is stolen by an alien who is up to no good." De La Soul voiced their own animated characters in the show. When the alien first takes their music, directly from their recording studio, Mase throws records like they're ninja stars ("Forty-five . . . forty-five . . . twelve-inch!") while Dave uses his microphone to deliver a sonic blast. Alas, the trio needs the Titans' help. Filled with references to specific De La Soul songs and albums, and their song "Pain" playing during the climactic battle scene, the episode's message is clear. As the animated Maseo puts it, "Give us back our music, fool!"

The big turning point came in the summer of 2021, when Tommy Boy was acquired by Reservoir Media. A music publishing company founded in 2007 by CEO Golnar Khosrowshahi, Reservoir first focused on owning the publishing of movie scores and various popular music. It acquired the record label Chrysalis Records in 2019, building out a recorded music division within the company. Less than two months before it became a publicly traded company, Reservoir Media announced they had acquired Tommy Boy. *Variety* put the price at around $100 million. Reservoir would continue to market the Tommy Boy catalog, with A&R led by Faith Newman, who had been involved in the hip-hop business since 1987, when she worked at Def Jam while in college. She's best known for signing Nas to Columbia Records.

Khosrowshahi told *Fast Company* that the day Reservoir closed on the Tommy Boy deal, the first phone call they made was to De La Soul. Newman phrased it similarly to *Complex*: "When Reservoir acquired Tommy Boy, the first call we made was to De La Soul. . . . We vowed to bring their music to streaming."

Rell Lafargue, president and COO of Reservoir, told *Complex* figuring out a specific deal with De La Soul, something the group would find more favorable than the 2019 Tommy Boy streaming offer, took just a few days. "I think from day one we saw eye to eye." The deal put ownership of De La Soul's master recordings firmly in their own hands, and included a plan for ensuring all samples were cleared correctly. Reservoir would handle the marketing and distribution of the albums.

To get the music ready for reissue, both digitally and physically, the company started the nearly two-year process of working with De La Soul, their manager Brandon Hixon, and their attorney Julian Petty to identify and find the proper rights holders for each sample used. They were "going through things one by one and addressing every situation," Khosrowshahi said to *Fast Company*. "It took patience and stamina." Lafargue told *Complex* that it was De La Soul who went to the rights holders to ask. Deborah Mannis-Gardner of DMG Clearances, who worked with De La on *Anonymous*, helped them navigate getting the clearances from the rights holders.

Some of the samples were not able to be cleared, and some were "too astronomically expensive" to be worth the effort, Maseo told Radio Milwaukee. De La Soul reunited with Prince Paul and engineer Scotty Hard, who worked on *De La Soul Is Dead*. For any sample they weren't going to clear, they needed to figure out a solution. That's where Prince Paul and Scotty Hard came in. For some, they left the sample out of the song, and tried to make the absence inconspicuous. Others involved the intense work of reworking the sample: replaying it without using the original recording, in a way that listeners hopefully wouldn't notice. It was "a whole lot of work in a short amount of time," Prince Paul told *Tape Op* magazine. They tried to use the same equipment as on the original recordings. They redid some of the scratches, but most of the original ones stayed.

The most noticeable differences in the reissues were on the album with the most samples: *3 Feet High and Rising*. "Cool Breeze on the Rocks" is essentially erased. The listener hears a backward record scratch in place of the jam-packed series of samples on the original. It's now titled "Cool Breeze on the Rocks (Melted Version)"; the records all melted away. "Magic Number" is missing the Eddie Murphy "hit by a car" sample. "Eye Know" has a "featuring" credit for Otis Redding, the result of their negotiations with his estate (across the albums there are other minor changes in how the tracks are titled). There are a few voices that seem replaced on "Jenifa Taught Me" and "Ghetto Thang." *Buhloone*'s "En Focus" has rerecorded vocals at the start. On *Stakes Is High*, there are some small elements missing, like a Run-D.M.C. sample on "Brakes" and the sample of Craig Mack speaking that opens "The Bizness." Fans will no doubt be figuring out differences for many years to come.

The reissued albums were released on streaming, and on vinyl, CD, and cassette, with the physical releases spread out over several months. It was what everyone had been waiting for—but the celebration had a bittersweet tone. Less than three weeks before De La Soul's first six albums would appear on streaming services, Dave Jolicoeur passed away, at age fifty-four. No cause of death was announced, but it was assumed to be related to his struggles with congestive heart failure. Pos and Maseo have shared in interviews that they knew of Dave's health issues but were shocked by his death; they had spoken to him two days before.

Lafargue told *Complex* that March 3, 2023, had been the goal for the streaming launch, and wasn't going to change, even though De La Soul and everyone involved was in a state of shock. Instead, the March 3 celebration would also become a tribute to the legacy of Dave. "We're doing this for Dave . . . when all of his music hits streaming services, I think people are going to have the opportunity to really continue to appreciate De La Soul, appreciate Dave and everything that he's done."

The combination of Dave's passing and the first six albums hitting streaming services led to more press attention for De La Soul than they'd had in a long time. And 2023 continued to be a busy touring year for De La Soul—just as an unexpected duo, paying tribute to their absent third partner as they performed. On the *People's Party with Talib Kweli* podcast, Posdnuos and Mase shared that when the trio talked two days before Dave passed, they were joking around as usual. They did talk about adjustments they'd need to make to the stage show so that Dave could continue to perform. They also discussed business matters and came to some agreements that helped ensure the De La Soul legacy would carry on. "A lot of things got really solid in the last forty-eight hours," Mase said.

They also confirmed in that podcast interview, and others, that they plan to keep performing and making music as De La Soul. They've said they don't have a stockpile of unreleased Trugoy vocals, yet there will be more new De La records. That might mean finally releasing Art Official Intelligence 3. It might mean releasing the Premium Soul on the Rocks album, produced by Pete Rock and DJ Premier, that they've talked about for years. It might mean something completely unexpected and new.

As Mase said, "Behind all this pain, creativity does flourish."

13. UP IN MY HEAD RIGHT NOW: A CONCLUSION

February 12, 2024—one year after David Jolicoeur's passing—Pos posted to Facebook and Instagram a photo of a smiling Dave. The words accompanying the post expressed conflicting feelings; Dave didn't like it when the day of someone's passing was used as commemoration. Yet the day felt important to those left behind. Like De La Soul's career itself, Pos's tribute was truly about the day-to-day work, the experience of those still here. He wrote, "To be clear I miss him in the physical everyday, rep for him everyday & will talk to someone about him everyday."

There's an under-heard De La Soul song from 1998, "Trouble in the Water" by DJ Honda, that starts with Dave saying, "What's up, world?" before mentioning he's about to "spread a little love to some folks who are up in my head right now." Over a groovy ECM Records jazz track, he recounts memories from childhood, of a friend and his mom who looked out for them; when she passed, it "hit me dead on my heart." The chorus is like a cousin to "Tread Water" from *3 Feet High and Rising*—water can get troubled in the blink of an eye; the way to keep afloat is to rely on the helping hands of others.

Tributes to loved ones are spread across De La Soul's discography. Their first single "Plug Tunin'" included the inscription "Dedicated to the memory of Hattie Mercer" on the record. That's Posdnuos's mother, the "pretty woman named Hattie" he referenced in "I Am I Be," where he observes that she "departed life just a little too soon / and didn't see me grab the Plug Tune fame."

The liner notes to the *Anonymous Nobody* album, their final recording as of the start of 2024, include Pos's tribute to two friends who passed: Phife from A Tribe Called Quest and DJ Timbuck2, a Chicago DJ who died at thirty-four of kidney cancer.

Many ghosts haunt the music and career of De La Soul. This slim book you hold in your hand mentions dozens of individuals who contributed in some way to this story and have passed away since De La Soul formed. At the least, there's all the following: John "Mr. Magic" Rivas, Biz Markie (Marcel Theo Hall), Prince Markie Dee (Mark Morales), Mike Joliceur, Robert Ford Jr., Don Newkirk, Anthony Ian "Poetic" Berkeley, James Brown, Lumumba "Professor X" Carson, Sonny Carson, Jeff Foss, Malik "Phife Dawg" Taylor, Greg Tate, Maggie Thrett, Melvin Bliss, Eric "Eazy-E" Wright, Michael Jackson, Sylvester Covin, John D. Loudermilk, Dave "Funken" Klein, Chris Lighty, Malcolm McLaren, Wilson Pickett, Gene Clark, Busta "Cherry" Jones, Daniel Dumile a.k.a. Zev Love X a.k.a. MF Doom, Pee Wee Ellis, Melvin Parker, Frank Wess, Keith "Guru" Elam, Lou Rawls, David Axelrod, Snooky Pryor, Eddie Harris, Jimmy Ponder, Tupac Shakur, Christopher Wallace a.k.a. Notorious B.I.G., James "J Dilla" Yancey, Nathaniel Hale a.k.a. Nate Dogg, Jonathan "Wordsayer" Moore, Timothy "Timbuk2" Jones, Fudge, Hattie Mercer, and David Jude "Trugoy" Joliceur. There's no chance that list is exhaustive. Rest in peace, one and all.

De La Soul's history—and hip-hop's—is riddled with the memories of human beings who've passed on from this earth. They depart and leave their essence behind. They're reborn, in a sense, every time their name and legacy are evoked. Hip-hop itself is built out of the births, deaths, and rebirths of music. Pop songs disappear from circulation and are reborn within hip-hop songs. The De La Soul trajectory is one of creative births, deaths, and rebirths. The daisies are born, the daisies die, something new is planted in their place. Native Tongues friendships form, dissolve, reemerge.

In 2024, De La Soul are in the middle of a rebirth of attention. After years of public invisibility, their music is comparatively everywhere. On February 12, the day after the Super Bowl, their song "The Magic Number" appeared in an online Adidas ad commemorating Kansas City Chiefs quarterback Patrick Mahomes winning three Super Bowls. On February 27, Pos and Maseo rang the bell at the New York Stock Exchange, along with their partners in Reservoir Media. It was in celebration of the thirty-fifth anniversary of *3 Feet High and Rising*, which was released in a deluxe streaming edition, with bonus tracks, in March. It included two rough demos from back in Mase's basement, a reminder of where it all began.

This current rebirth of De La Soul has been about celebrating a legacy and making it both available and evident to new audiences. Yet even during the non-streaming years, the influence of their music was clear. De La Soul played a significant role in the musical and emotional widening of hip-hop, and in spreading its influence overseas. It's not a stretch to trace a line from the Native Tongues' camaraderie through to the Hieroglyphics and the Dungeon Family, to Pharrell and the Neptunes, to Odd Future and Black Hippy. Or to take the jazz and jazz-adjacent musicians of the current era who grew up on hip-hop and find specific connecting points to De La Soul and their compadres—especially Dilla's approach to rhythm and Tribe's jazz-inflected *Low End Theory* album. Guitarist Jeff Parker, pianist Vijay Iyer, flutist Tenderlonious, bassist Junius Paul, and drummer Moses Boyd are just a few examples of current-day jazz players who have given interviews or made social media posts where they mention De La Soul as an influence or at least a fixture of their musical upbringings. You can hear it in how they play with openness and exploration that dances in, out, and around hip-hop itself.

What comes next for De La Soul as a group will transcend nostalgia for their decades-old records. Don't bet against them surprising everyone with their next move, given the dedication to their creative instincts that has brought them this far. There is a video clip that sometimes shows up on YouTube, from an interview De La Soul did with Sista Dee Barnes on *Pump It Up* in 1991, soon after the release of *De La Soul Is Dead.* In it, Maseo outlined their approach to each successive project: "We always said that we was always gonna do something new on each album . . . we kinda feel to stay in it, you gotta change every time."

Even in 2024, close to four decades after some Long Island teenagers started messing around with records in their basements, De La Soul seem ready to "stay in it." Like the song says, "De La to the death."

ACKNOWLEDGMENTS

The biggest thank-you I can offer is to De La Soul and Prince Paul, for their creativity and the ample number of interviews they gave writers and podcasters over the past thirty-five years. If they hadn't been as generous and open, this book would not have been possible. Thanks also to every interviewer and writer mentioned in this book—superheroes all, for their devotion to chronicling the development, legacy, and impact of hip-hop.

Thanks to Jeff Gomez and J-Card Press for asking me to write a book, and encouraging my choice of topic, and to all editors who've provided homes for my writing over the years (especially Sarah Zupko Kondeusz, Karen Zarker, and Jack Rabid).

A heartfelt thanks to my wife, Jill, and my sons, Miles and Graeme, for giving me the support and time to get this accomplished. And to friends, especially the KC Music Trivia crowd, for indulging my need to talk with people about music.

DE LA SOUL

Lastly, recognition for all the public places where I worked on writing this book, for being welcoming spaces with atmosphere and Wi-Fi: multiple branches of three library systems (Kansas City Public Library, Johnson County Library, Mid-Continent Public Library), Kansas City Zoo, Alma Mader Brewing, Boulevard Beer Hall, Front Range Café, and multiple locations of the Roasterie Coffee Company.

CHAPTER NOTES

1. Bigger than Me: An introduction
"De La Soul's Maseo Talks about Losing Band Member Trugoy and Continuing the Band." Interview by Lyndsey Parker. Yahoo Entertainment. July 25, 2023. Video, 6:23. https://youtu.be/xvswBq9UOsM.

2. Different, but Dope: Youth culture and the members of De La Soul
Hart, Ron. "'Beat Street': The Making of a Hip-Hop Classic." *Wondering Sound*, August 15, 2014. http://www.wonderingsound.com/feature/beat-street-movie-oral-history, archived August 21, 2014, at the Wayback Machine.

Klaess, John. *Breaks in the Air: The Birth of Rap Radio in New York City*. Durham: Duke University Press, 2022.

Rakim. *Sweat the Technique*. New York: Amistad, 2020.

"Prince Paul Interview: Legendary Rap Pioneer and De La Soul Producer | Ep. 46." Interview by Kambi Thandi. *The Crate 808 Hip Hop Podcast*. April 25, 2020. Video, 1:30. https://youtu.be/jszr5q1et1Q.

Caramanica, John, and Joe Coscarelli, "50 Rappers, 50 Stories." *New York Times*, July 18, 2023. https://www.nytimes.com/interactive/2023/07/18/arts/music/hiphop50.html.

George, Nelson. *Buppies, B-boys, Baps, and Bohos: Notes on Post-Soul Black Culture*. New York: Perennial, 1992.

DE LA SOUL

"Maseo Talks De La Soul, Sampling and Dilla." Interview by Cognito. Red Bull Music Academy. April 18, 2018. Video, 1:30. https://youtu.be/7w3vkUWzGq4.

"Damien Lil D Morgan Interviews Maseo of De La Soul for Hip Hop Had a Dream." Interview by Damien "Lil D" Morgan. Dynamexx-TV. Recorded May 19, 2005. Published May 17, 2011. Video, 8:30. https://youtu.be/B6ABEl0FLn8.

Hewitt, Paolo. "De La Soul: Soul Deep High and Rising." *New Musical Express*, April 1, 1989.

Rabin, Nathan. "De La Soul." *A.V. Club*, August 9, 2000. https://www.avclub.com/de-la-soul-1798208102.

Earls, John. "De La Soul: 'Three Black Men Staying Together for So Long Is Beautiful and Important.'" *Classic Pop Magazine*, June 7, 2022. https://www.classicpopmag.com/2022/06/de-la-soul-interview/.

"DJ Maseo—Deep Friendship with Prince Paul & How We Connected for De La Soul." Interview. 247HH. March 8, 2018. Video, 7:28. https://youtu.be/oMzdsaiAtuM.

Brown, Ethan. "My Name is Prince . . . and I Make Beats." *The Source*, April 1999.

"Unscripted with Prince Paul." Interview by Matt Perry. *Serato Unscripted*. September 6, 2022. Video, 1:27. https://youtu.be/rTjRETlToK4.

Mason, Andrew. "The Memoirs of Prince Paul." *Wax Poetics*, Spring 2002.

Cipha Sounds and Peter Rosenberg. "Ep#30: Finally, De La Soul on *Juan Ep*!" *Juan Epstein (Juan Ep Is Life)*. Podcast audio. October 13, 2015. https://audioboom.com/posts/3687830-finally-de-la-soul-on-juan-ep.

"Daddy O—How Stetsasonic Got a Deal & Why We Signed with Tommy Boy." Interview. 247HH. November 24, 2016. Video, 6:18. https://youtu.be/YgNbWUtJdz4.

Ford Jr., Robert. "B-Beats Bombarding Bronx: Mobile DJ Starts

Something with Oldie R&B Disks." In *That's the Joint!: The Hip-Hop Studies Reader*, eds. Murray Forman and Mark Anthony Neal, 41–43. New York: Routledge, 2016.

Mao, Jeff. "Across 135th Street with Guest Monica Lynch." *Across 135th Street*. Podcast audio. April 17, 2018. https://soundcloud.com/chairmanmaonyc/across-135th-street-monica-lynch.

Charnas, Dan. *The Big Payback: The History of the Business of Hip-Hop*. New York: Berkley Books, 2011.

Proctor, Ryan. "Old to the New Q&A (Part One)—Daddy-O." *Old to the New*, September 1, 2013. https://oldtothenew.wordpress.com/2013/09/01/old-to-the-new-qa-part-one-daddy-o/.

Fitzmaurice, Larry. "5-10-15-20: Prince Paul." *Pitchfork*, October 25, 2012. https://pitchfork.com/features/5-10-15-20/8975-prince-paul/.

"DJ Maseo on His Start in New York, De La Soul and the Music Industry." Interview by Matt Perry. *Serato Unscripted*. July 2, 2019. Video, 1:21:54. https://youtu.be/fTiB_yVHHjo.

Open Mike Eagle. "3ft High and Rising: The Origins of De La Soul." *What Had Happened Was*. Podcast audio. July 8, 2020.

"Interview—DJ Maseo of De La Soul." Interview by DJ Frenic. dBs Institute. February 12, 2016. Video, 1:01:35. https://youtu.be/xwJIVrEpn5I.

Ogg, Alex, and David Upshal. *The Hip Hop Years: A History of Rap*. New York: Fromm, 2001.

Coleman, Brian. Check the Technique: Liner Notes for Hip-Hop Junkies. New York: Villard, 2007.

"Prince Paul Talks Forming De La Soul and Sampling." Interview by Torsten Schmidt. Red Bull Music Academy. July 15, 2017. Video, 30:33. https://youtu.be/wOEgVdL6cSw.

Ettelson, Robbie. "DJ Stitches—the *Unkut* Interview." Unkut.com. February 14, 2018. https://unkut.com/2014/02/dj-stitches-the-unkut-interview/.

3. Believe What We Believe: Getting started, getting signed, and the first singles

"Maseo Talks." Red Bull Music Academy.

Coleman, Brian. *Rakim Told Me: Wax Facts Straight from the Original Artists—the '80s*. New York: Wax Facts Press, 2005.

Ma, David. "The Kool Keith Interview." *Medium*, August 22, 2021. https://davidma1.medium.com/the-kool-keith-interview-c7b96c73b6bf.

De La Soul. "The Delacratic Dictionary." In *Frank151—De La Soul: Chapter 37*. New York: Frank151 Media Group, 2009.

"De La Soul: The Current State of Hip Hop Is Redundant." Interview by Trevor Nelson. BBC Radio 1Xtra. July 15, 2016. Video, 6:29. https://youtu.be/Huj5oPlG2EY.

"De La Soul on Trugoy the Dove, Music Ownership, Hip Hop's Evolution, New Album & More | Drink Champs." Interview by N.O.R.E. and DJ EFN. Revolt.TV. June 10, 2023. Video, 2:42. https://youtu.be/DaIrsMM2oqY.

"DJ Maseo—Deep Friendship with Prince Paul & How We Connected for De La Soul." Interview. 247HH. March 8, 2018. Video, 7:28. https://youtu.be/oMzdsaiAtuM.

Coleman. *Check the Technique*.

Abrams, Jonathan. *The Come Up: An Oral History of the Rise of Hip-Hop*. New York: Crown, 2022.

Ogg and Upshal. *The Hip Hop Years*.

Gonzales, Michael A. "De La Soul Is (Not) Dead." *Ebony*, September 2016.

"Building, 1989–1991: The Untold Story of a Lost New York City Hip Hop Club," Standard Hotels, published July 29, 2016, https://www.standardhotels.com/culture/Building-Hip-Hop-NYC-De-La-Soul-Tribe-Called-Quest.

Ross, Dante. *Son of the City: A Memoir*. New York: Rare Bird Books, 2023.

Cipha Sounds and Peter Rosenberg. "Ep #30."

Ross, Dante. "Rap De Rap Show." In *Frank151—De La Soul: Chapter 37*, 40–44. New York: Frank151 Media Group, 2009.

Tate, Greg. *Flyboy in the Buttermilk: Essays on Contemporary America*. New York: Simon & Schuster, 1992.

Busch, Robbie. "Back to the Future." *Wax Poetics*, October/November 2006.

Huntley, Daniel. "Walking Tall with Kevin Bray." *Shots*, July 11, 2017. https://www.shots.net/news/view/walking-tall-with-kevin-bray.

4. Eyes Wide Open: *3 Feet High and Rising* and the D.A.I.S.Y. Age
Cipha Sounds and Peter Rosenberg. "Ep #30."

"De La Soul | Drink Champs." Interview by N.O.R.E. and DJ EFN. Revolt.TV. March 29, 2019. Video, 1:50:00. https://youtu.be/jsv1R3PrGAU.

Coleman. *Check the Technique*.

"Prince Paul Talks." Red Bull Music Academy.

Brodhagen, Tim. "Calliope." In *Frank151—De La Soul: Chapter 37*, 61–67. New York: Frank151 Media Group, 2009.

Rossi, Dana. "Mellini Kantayya Interviews Plug One from De La Soul." Soundtrack Series, June 28, 2013. https://www.soundtrackseries.com/blog/2013/06/28/mellini-kantayya-interviews-plug-one-from-de-la-soul/, archived October 15, 2013, at the Wayback Machine.

Patrin, Nate. *Bring That Beat Back: How Sampling Built Hip-Hop*. Minneapolis: University of Minnesota Press, 2022.

Dery, Mark. "Digital Underground, Coldcut and De La Soul Jam the Beat." *Keyboard*, March 1991.

Serpick, Evan. "'3 Feet High and Rising': De La Soul's Track by Track Guide to Groundbreaking 1989 LP." *Rolling Stone*, June 3, 2009.

Cho, Jaeki. "Prince Paul Tells All: The Stories Behind His Classic

DE LA SOUL

Records (Part 1)." *Complex*, December 8, 2011. https://www.complex.com/music/a/jaeki-cho/prince-paul-tells-all-the-stories-behind-his-classic-records-part-1.

Weiss, Jeff. "A History of the Hip Hop Skit." *Red Bull Music Academy Daily*, July 7, 2015. https://daily.redbullmusicacademy.com/2015/07/hip-hop-skits-history.

Batey, Angus. "The Magic Number: The Story of *3 Feet High and Rising*." *HipHop.com*, April 7, 2009. Republished March 4, 2019. https://thequietus.com/articles/26140-de-la-soul-3-feet-high-and-rising-review-anniversary.

De La Soul. "De La's Pop Quiz." In *Frank151—De La Soul: Chapter 37*, 150–52. New York: Frank151 Media Group, 2009.

Open Mike Eagle. "*3 Feet High . . .*"

"Artist on Artist: Posdnuos of De La Soul Talks to Rhymefest." *Chicago Reader*, May 27, 2012. https://chicagoreader.com/film/artist-on-artist-posdnuos-of-de-la-soul-talks-to-rhymefest/.

Breannan, Neal, and Moshe Kasher. "Maseo from De La Soul." *The Champs*. Podcast audio. January 29, 2014.

Simpson, Dave. "How We Made *3 Feet High and Rising*." *The Guardian*, April 29, 2014. https://www.theguardian.com/music/2014/apr/29/how-we-made-3-feet-high-and-rising-de-la-soul.

Mott, Toby. "New York City, Hip Hop in the Daisy Age, Summer 1989." Hypergallery.com. https://hypergallery.com/en-us/blogs/blog/new-york-city-hip-hop-in-the-daisy-age-summer-1989.

"DJ Maseo." *Serato Unscripted*.

Clinton, George, with Ben Freeman. *Brothas Be, Yo Like George, Ain't That Funkin' Kinda Hard on You?* New York: Atria, 2017.

"Celebrating De La Soul, with Questlove." *Popcast*. New York Times podcast audio, March 8, 2023.

Christgau, Robert. "New Kids on the Block." *Village Voice*, February 27, 1990. Republished at www.robertchristgau.com/xg/pnj/pj89.php.

Azerrad, Michael. "De La Soul: *3 Feet High and Rising*." *Rolling Stone*, March 23, 1989.

Cromelin, Rochard. "Pop Review: Mythology, Metaphysics of De La Soul." *Los Angeles Times*, May 31, 1989. https://www.latimes.com/archives/la-xpm-1989-05-31-ca-825-story.html.

Harrington, Richard. "De La Soul's Mind-Bending Rap." *Washington Post*, May 18, 1989.

Stubbs, David. "De La Soul: The D.A.I.S.Y. Chain Gang." *Melody Maker*, June 10, 1989.

Push. "De La Soul: Space Cadets." *Melody Maker*, April 8, 1989.

"De La Soul Interview with *The Breakfast Club*." Interview by DJ Envy, Angela Yee, and Charlemagne the God. *The Breakfast Club*. August 25, 2016. Video, 27:46. https://youtu.be/onWS20ejGMU.

O'Hagan, Sean. "De La Soul: Brothers from Another Planet." *New Musical Express*, October 21, 1989.

Sullivan, Jim. "De La Soul: Venus de Milo, Boston MA." *Boston Globe*, May 1989.

Azerrad, Michael. "De La Soul's Hippie-hop: Psychedelic Rappers Introduce the DA.I.S.Y. Age." *Rolling Stone*, May 4, 1989.

"Sir Mix-A-Lot and DJ Maseo Visit the *Barbershop*—Episode 115." Interview by T-Holla and Tru. *The Barbershop Show*. December 8, 2015. Video, 24:41. https://youtu.be/vogDLjksnWk.

HeadKrack. "De La Soul Full Interview 2015 Retro Hours." Interview. Recorded May 4, 2015. Published February 16, 2023. Video, 23:59. https://youtu.be/4-OTQtmE0N4.

Murphy, Keith. "Phife Dawg: Memories of Native Tongues' Five Foot Assassin." *Vibe*, March 23, 2016. https://www.vibe.com/music/music-news/phife-dawg-tribe-called-quest-tribute-interview-412449/.

5. Shades of Black Complexity: The Native Tongues collective
Nelson, Jill. "A Proud Fashion Statement." *Washington Post*, April 28, 1989. https://www.washingtonpost.com/archive/local/1989/04/28/a-

proud-fashion-statement/adb512bb-fcd1-455b-a69d-2647abe4f1ad/.

O'Hagan, Sean. "De La Soul: Brothers from Another Planet."

Chang, Jeff. *Can't Stop Won't Stop: A History of the Hip-Hop Generation*. New York: Picador, 2005.

Scott, Dana. "De La Soul Details Native Tongues Formation, Standout Cut 'Buddy.'" *HopHopDX*, July 29, 2014. https://hiphopdx.com/news/id.29939/title.de-la-soul-details-native-tongues-formation-standout-cut-buddy.

"Talib Kweli & Monie Love Talk 'Monie in the Middle,' Native Tongues, Jean Grae | People's Party." Interview by Talib Kweli and Jasmin Leigh. UPROXX Video. August 10, 2020. Video, 1:11:12. https://youtu.be/k1Yosw0f1bE.

Coleman, Brian. *Check the Technique, Volume 2: More Liner Notes for Hip-Hop Junkies*. Berkeley: Gingko Press / Wax Facts Press, 2014.

Ettelson, Robbie. "DJ Johnny Juice and Son of Bazerk—the *Unkut* Interview." Unkut.com. May 13, 2008. https://unkut.com/2008/05/dj-johnny-juice-and-son-of-bazerk-the-unkut-interview/.

Saleh, Oumar. "We've Got a File on You: DJ Shadow." *Stereogum*. October 26, 2023. https://www.stereogum.com/2240398/dj-shadow-new-album-unkle-dj-hero-rare-records/interviews/weve-got-a-file-on-you/.

"Q-Tip Talks Prince, Native Tongues, Missing Phife, and the Future of the Music Business." Interview by Jon Fortt. *Fortt Knox*. June 25, 2018. Video, 52:49. https://youtu.be/5yyNMpxpY54.

6. Trying to Still Live: Controlling the narrative through *De La Soul Is Dead*

Kauffman, Leah. "John Oates on His New Album, Rock and Roll Hall of Fame Induction, and What 'I Can't Go for That' Is Really About." *Philadelphia Inquirer*, March 18, 2014. https://www.inquirer.com/philly/entertainment/music/John_Oates_on_his_new_album_Rock_and_Roll_Hall_of_Fame_induction_and_what_I_Cant_Go_For_That_is_really_about_.html

Owen, Frank. "Sampling: Bite This." *Spin*, November 1989. https://

www.spin.com/2021/05/bite-this-1989-sampling-feature/.

Clinton with Freeman. *Brothas Be, Yo Like George.*

Ogg and Upshal. *The Hip Hop Years.*

Kayman, Howard. *Shell Shocked: My Life with the Turtles Flo and Eddie and Frank Zappa*, Etc. Minneapolis: University of Minnesota Press, 2013.

Dafoe, Chris. "De La Soul Wraps Up Its Sound for Stage." *Toronto Star*, February 16, 1990.

DJ Sorce-1. "Reconstructing the De La Soul Years with Prince Paul (Part Two)," Smoking Section, August 21, 2008. http://smokingsection.uproxx.com:80/TSS/2008/08/reconstructing-the-de-la-soul-years-with-prince-paul-part-two, archived April 16, 2009, at the Wayback Machine.

Open Mike Eagle. "De La Soul Is Dead." *What Had Happened Was*. Podcast audio. August 5, 2020.

"Vinia Mojica: The Hip-Hop Troubadour Tells Her Story." *The Revivalist*, February 28, 2012. https://kalamu.posthaven.com/audio-interview-vinia-mojica-the-hip-hop-trou.

"Le'Shaun: Background Story of Making the Hit Record "Monie in the Middle" with Monie Love (Part 5)." Interview by Nnamdi Okoye. *Halftime Chat*, July 7, 2023. Video, 11:06. https://youtu.be/KqqS5vWLki4.

Daly, Steven. "Cool Hip Hop: De La Soul De-flowered." *Spin*, May 1991.

Kenner, Rob. "De La Soul Picks Their Favorite (and/or Most Hated) Tracks." *GQ*, February 27, 2023. https://www.gq.com/story/de-la-soul-albums-streaming-favorite-songs-dave-jolicoeur-trugoy-the-dove.

Nicely, J. "Say No Go." In *Frank151—De La Soul: Chapter 37*, 143–48. New York: Frank151 Media Group, 2009.

ATCO. "De La Soul Is Dead." *The Source*, May 1991. Republished at https://ifihavent.wordpress.com/2007/04/20/classic-review-de-la-soul-is-dead-in-the-source-1991/.

Reynolds, Simon. "De La Soul: Malice in Wonderland." *Melody Maker*, May 25, 1991.

Considine, J. D. "De La Soul: De La Soul Is Dead." *Musician*, July 1991.

Pareles, Jon. "Pop Music: Is De La Soul Dead, or Just Too Famous?" *New York Times*, May 12, 1991.

McMillen, Andrew. "The Vine Interview: Posdnuos of De La Soul." *The Vine*, February 8, 2011. https://www.thevine.com.au/music/interviews/de-la-soul-_-interview20110207.aspx.

Simpson, Dave. "De La Soul on Their Belated Streaming Debut: 'It felt like we were being erased from history.'" *The Guardian*, February 23, 2023. https://www.theguardian.com/music/2023/feb/23/de-la-soul-interview-belated-streaming-debut.

"Questlove Talks De La Soul and Real Hip-Hop." Interview by Andrew Mason. Red Bull Music Academy. Recorded 2005, published May 14, 2014. Video, 2:12:56. https://youtu.be/acq54q3r96I.

Light, Alan. "New Faces of 1991: De La Soul." *Rolling Stone*, April 18, 1991.

7. Through the Machine: *Buhloone Mindstate* and growing up
"De La Soul on Dashikis Being Cool, HipHop Nerds & Smacking Cats, Writing Raps + New Album." August 24, 2016. Interview by Ebro and Laura Stylez. Hot 97. Video, 35:15, https://www.youtube.com/watch?v=HsWEMnZpj-0&t=43s.

Wang, Oliver. "20 Years Ago, De La Soul Refused to Go Pop." NPR, December 30, 2013. https://www.npr.org/sections/thereco rd/2013/12/30/258155415/20-years-ago-de-la-soul-refused-to-go-pop.

"Sucka Free Stogie Show Ep. 4 w/ DJ Maseo." *Sucka Free Stogie Show*, February 9, 2017. Video, 28:51. https://youtu.be/FYEQD9YPvB4. Kenner, Rob. "De La Soul Picks."

Journalist Sin-Seer. "History Lesson Ep. 167 Part 1 with Shortie No Mas." December 18, 2021. Video, 23:54. https://youtu.

be/9X4_04DFKdc.

"DJ Maseo—Working on "Buhloone Mindstate" with the J.B.'s." Interview. 247HH. March 15, 2018. Video, 4:07. https://youtu.be/ARFcPV0LeKQ.

"How Does De La Soul Sound in the Streaming Era?" NPR All Songs Considered. March 14, 2023. https://www.npr.org/2023/03/13/1163189729/how-does-de-la-soul-sound-in-the-streaming-era.

Smith, Danyel. "Classic Reviews: De La Soul, 'Buhloone Mindstate.'" *Spin*, August 4, 2023. https://www.spin.com/2023/08/de-la-soul-buhloone-mindstate-album-review.

"DJ Maseo." *Serato Unscripted*.

Wang, Oliver. "Buhloone Bonus Beats." *Soul Sides*, December 30, 2013. https://soul-sides.com/2013/12/buhloone-bonus-beats.html.

"Let the Record Show—Episode 1: Talib Kweli Interview." Interview by Mike Pizzo and Warren Peace. *Let the Record Show.* November 18, 2016. Video, 30:29. https://youtu.be/liR6c62esc4.

Washington Post Staff. "50 Hip-Hop Artists Share 50 Songs They Love." *Washington Post*, August 4, 2023. https://www.washingtonpost.com/arts-entertainment/interactive/2023/hip-hop-50-years-anniversary-playlist.

Weingarten, Christopher. "Oral History of the 'Judgment Night' Soundtrack: 1993's Rap-Rock Utopia." *Rolling Stone*, September 13, 2018. https://www.rollingstone.com/music/music-features/judgment-night-soundtrack-oral-history-1993-rap-rock-summit-722094.

Weiss, Jeff. "A Conversation with Posdnuos of De La Soul: On Nike Run Mixes, the Current State of Hip-Hop and Oodles of O's." *L.A. Weekly*, April 30, 2009. https://www.laweekly.com/a-conversation-with-posdnuos-of-de-la-soul-on-nike-run-mixes-the-current-state-of-hip-hop-and-oodles-of-os.

8. What's Going On: The turning point that was *Stakes Is High*
Open Mike Eagle. "Buhloone Mindstate." *What Had Happened Was*. Podcast audio. September 9, 2020.

DE LA SOUL

"De La Soul: The World Cafe Interview." Interview by Stephen Kallao. *World Cafe*, August 4, 2023. Video, 34:00. https://youtu.be/1BsYk9HQkB8.

Houghton, Eddie "Stats." "In Their Own Words: De La Soul Reveals the Secret History of 'Stakes Is High.'" *Okayplayer*, July 2016. Republished January 5, 2023. https://www.okayplayer.com/originals/de-la-soul-stakes-is-high.html

"DJ Maseo." *Serato Unscripted*.

Muro, Matt. "De La Soul's Spirit Didn't Need City Streets," *New York Times*, August 13, 2000. https://www.nytimes.com/2000/08/13/nyregion/de-la-soul-s-spirit-didn-t-need-city-streets.html.
Kenner, Rob. "De La Soul Picks."

Hernandez, Victoria. "De La Soul Explains Who Is Carrying 'Stakes Is High' Legacy on 20th Anniversary of Album." *HopHopDX*, July 1, 2016. https://hiphopdx.com/news/id.39452/title.de-la-soul-explains-who-is-carrying-stakes-is-high-legacy-on-20th-anniversary-of-album.

Hasted, Nick. "De La Soul: Reissues." *Uncut*, July 2003.

"De La Soul on . . ." Revolt.TV.

9. That New-Millennium Feel: The *Art Official Intelligence* "trilogy"

"De La Soul." Revolt.TV.

Hall, Rashaun. "De La Soul Bows Triple-CD Project." *Billboard*, July 15, 2000.

Brannan, Eddie. "De La Soul's Endless Rebirths." *The Fader*, Summer 2000. Republished online February 14, 2023. https://www.thefader.com/2023/02/14/cover-story-de-la-souls-endless-rebirths.

Pizzo. "De La Soul Speaks on *Art Official Intelligence*." HipHopSite.com, January 1, 2000. http://www.hiphopsite.com/2000/01/01/de-la-soul-speaks-on-art-official-intelligence.

Shabazz, Sherron. "A Conversation with Supa Dave West." *The Real Hip-Hop*, November 7, 2016. https://therealhip-hop.com/a-conversation-with-supa-dave-west.

"DJ Maseo—Racist Turkish Gang Beat Me Up & Tried To Kill Me." Interview. 247HH, March 18, 2018. Video, 8:51. https://youtu.be/zjuDAIhvqHs.

"De La Soul Talk Making "Stakes Is High," Native Tongues, and Losing David Jolicoeur | People's Party." Interview by Talib Kweli. UPROXX Video. August 28, 2023. Video, 47:53. https://youtu.be/ZZs7iVGvRcA.

Christgau, Robert. "De La Soul Consumer Guide Reviews." https://www.robertchristgau.com/get_artist.php?name=De+La+Soul.

10. Legacy Lives On: Industry turmoil, *Grind Date*, and Gorillaz
"De La Soul Posdnuos Interview." MVRemix, May 26, 2016. Audio, 14:45. https://youtu.be/h-P5h4YJZoo?si=c1vhAQM3i__DV3-8.

Ma, David. "The Making of De La Soul's 'Rock Co.Kane Flow' Featuring MF Doom." *Passion of the Weiss*, August 6, 2020. https://www.passionweiss.com/2020/08/06/the-making-of-de-la-souls-rock-co-kane-flow-featuring-mf-doom.

Drum Broker. "Jake One—Behind the Beat (De La Soul—Rock Co.Kane Flow feat. MF DOOM)." June 23, 2013. Video, 5:39. https://youtu.be/aW_hx9Ao5rM?si=oGTBR-Mellkax-sS.

Sorcinelli, Gino. "Beats You Would Give Mobb Deep": Jake One Re-Examines "Rock Co.Kane Flow." *Medium*, July 13, 2017. https://medium.com/micro-chop/beats-you-would-give-mobb-deep-jake-one-deconstructs-rock-co-kane-flow-844399028888.

"DJ Maseo—Working with the Gorillaz & Significance of Twilite Tone to "Humanz." Interview. 247HH, April 3, 2018. Video, 6:40. https://youtu.be/LcF2Ld9Rpeo.

11. Stars Unleashed: The digital void and the *Anonymous Nobody*
"Posdnuos Speaks on the Roots vs. De La Soul," Interview by Davey D. HardKnockTV. September 22, 2009. Video, 8:16. https://youtu.be/2i-UzXOfllE.

Wallace, Riley. "Interview with Dave aka Trugoy of De La Soul." *Above Average Hip-Hop*, April 27, 2015. http://aboveaveragehiphop.com/interview-with-dave-aka-trugoy-of-de-la-soul.

Radford, Chad. "De La Soul on the Long Road to Independence."

DE LA SOUL

Creative Loafing, April 13, 2015. https://creativeloafing.com/content-150081-de-la-soul-on-the-long-road-to.

Shabazz, Sherron. "A Conversation."

Setaro, Shawn. "How De La Soul Crowdfunded Their New Album with $600K from Kickstarter." *Forbes*, August 30, 2016. https://www.forbes.com/sites/shawnsetaro/2016/08/30/de-la-souls-kickstarter-success/?sh=4a77250d72b8.

McIntyre, Hugh. "These Are the Top 5 Most-Funded Music Kickstarter Campaigns." Forbes, April 13, 2015. https://www.forbes.com/sites/hughmcintyre/2015/04/13/these-are-the-top-5-most-funded-music-kickstarter-campaigns/?sh=1c920465d7e2.

"De La Soul Posdnuos Interview." *MVRemix*.

"Sir Mix-A-Lot and DJ Maseo." *The Barbershop Show*.

Diep, Eric. "De La Soul Talk New Album and Getting Snubbed by Willie Nelson." Complex, August 26, 2016. https://www.complex.com/music/a/eric-diep/de-la-soul-talk-new-album-getting-snubbed-by-willie-nelson.

Molanphy, Chris. Old Town Road. Durham: Duke University Press, 2023.

12. Creativity Does Flourish: Reissues, tragedy, and the future
Cohen, Finn. "De La Soul's Legacy Is Trapped in Digital Limbo." *New York Times*, August 9, 2016. https://www.nytimes.com/2016/08/14/arts/music/de-la-soul-digital-albums.html.

"De La Soul Is Getting Robbed by Tommy Boy Records Still on Their 30th Anniversary." Interview by Sway Calloway. Sway's Universe, February 26, 2019. Video, 46:10. https://youtu.be/XqOo8MCljeg.

Lamarre, Carl. "De La Soul On '3 Feet High & Rising' 30th Anniversary, Working with DJ Premier, Ongoing Battle with Tommy Boy." *Billboard*, March 4, 2019. https://www.billboard.com/music/rb-hip-hop/de-la-soul-interview-three-feet-and-rising-anniversary-tommy-boy-jay-z-8500860.

LaPorte, Nicole. "If You've Been Listening to De La Soul Lately, You

Probably Have Golnar Khosrowshahi to Thank." *Fast Company*, July 6, 2023. https://www.fastcompany.com/90910381/golnar-khosrowshahi-reservoir-media-de-la-soul.

Cummings-Grady, Mackenzie. "De La Soul's Music Catalog Begins Official Streaming Rollout with "The Magic Number." *Complex*, January 3, 2023. https://www.complex.com/music/a/mack/de-la-soul-music-catalog-coming-to-streaming-services.

"De La Soul's Maseo: 'The Dream Became Real Life and Kept Going.'" Interview by Dori Zori. Radio Milwaukee, April 24, 2023. Video, 33:32. https://youtu.be/_IpL-u9Ldvw?si=AS-ouXA83XiQGCyK.

Retzer, Sam. "Prince Paul: Happier Than Ever." *Tape Op*, November/December 2023. https://tapeop.com/interviews/158/prince-paul.

Rose, Jordan. "How De La Soul's Legendary Catalog Finally Made It to Streaming Platforms." *Complex*, March 3, 2023. https://www.complex.com/music/a/j-rose/de-la-soul-streaming-platforms-reservoir-interview.

"De La Soul." UPROXX Video.

Printed in the USA
CPSIA information can be obtained
at www.ICGtesting.com
LVHW091548070824
787583LV00008B/738